Angela Thomas

Stronger

Finding Hope in Fragile Places

LifeWay Press®
Nashville, Tennessee

Published by LifeWay Press®
© 2013 Angela Thomas
Reprinted April 2014

ISBN 9781415874141
Item 005513458.
Dewey decimal classification: 234.2
Subject headings: HOPE \ DISCIPLESHIP \ GOD

Unless indicated otherwise, all Scripture quotations are taken from the Holy Bible, English Standard Version, copyright © 2000, 2001 by Crossway Bibles, a division of Good News Publishers.

Scripture marked NIV is taken from the Holy Bible, NEW INTERNATIONAL VERSION®. Copyright © 1973, 1978, 1984 by Biblica, Inc. All rights reserved worldwide. Used by permission.

Scripture marked HCSB is taken from the Holman Christian Standard Bible. Copyright © 1999, 2000, 2002, 2003, 2009 by Holman Bible Publishers. Used by permission. Holman Christian Standard Bible® and HCSB® are federally registered trademarks of Holman Bible Publishers.

Scripture marked NASB is taken from the New American Standard Bible®, Copyright © 1960, 1962, 1963, 1968, 1971, 1972, 1973, 1975, 1977, 1995 by the Lockman Foundation. Used by permission *(www.lockman.org)*.

To order additional copies of this resource, write to LifeWay Church Resources, Customer Service, One LifeWay Plaza, Nashville, TN 37234-0113; fax 615.251.5933; phone 800.458.2772; order online at www.lifeway.com or email orderentry@lifeway.com; or visit the LifeWay Christian Store serving you.

Printed in the United States of America

Adult Ministry Publishing
LifeWay Church Resources
One LifeWay Plaza
Nashville, TN 37234-0152

CONTENTS

I love you, O Lord, my strength.

Psalm 18:1

ABOUT THE AUTHOR

Angela is a graduate of the University of North Carolina at Chapel Hill and Dallas Theological Seminary. She is the author of 15 books, including the best-selling *52 Things Kids Need from a Mom*. She has written six video studies with LifeWay, including **Brave: Honest Questions Women Ask**. As a sought-after Bible teacher, Angela brings her passion, transparency, and storytelling gifts to women of all ages and all walks of life from all around the world.

This life journey has not been without its challenges, darkness, and pain. After divorcing, Angela spent more than seven years as a single mom to her four children. You will find the lessons of brokenness, pain, and God's redemption woven throughout her writings. Angela is humbled that God continues to use her brokenness for His glory.

Over five years ago, God sent a man named Scott to marry Angela and her children. They live in North Carolina where their family loves travel, cooking at home, having people over, and going to church. Angela especially loves everything about making a home for her family, including cooking, decorating, gardening, and organizing.

The study is written. The videos are filmed. Only this last personal note remains to be written to you. I'm so humbled to have you spend your precious time with these pages. The study is a responsibility I do not take lightly. I've asked Christ to be the center of this work. I pray that He will be exalted in your life. I pray His presence will be real and powerful to you.

This study was not written by a strong woman in a strong season of life. God may have chosen the weakest woman on the planet. Only now with the writing complete have I begun to understand. I blocked several months on my calendar to write, but God had something more in mind. When the month came for me to begin writing, my parents came to live with our family. My mama had been battling ovarian cancer for almost six years. Both Mama and Daddy were completely exhausted. They lived with us, and we later moved them into a house down the street. Caring for someone who is desperately ill is all-consuming.

I anticipated months of writing. God anticipated the lessons I had yet to learn. Instead of research, exegesis and theology, God asked me to pull up a chair beside the bed of His presence. Everyday, He had me look into the bluest eyes you've ever seen, searching for ways to bring a moment of joy or relief from the pain. He asked me to serve Mama and my family until I was the most physically and emotionally exhausted I have ever been.

Long before we thought we were ready, and long before we had hoped, Mama went to heaven, where in His presence, and by His grace, she was finally and fully made strong. Afterward, in the middle of my grief, exhaustion, and weakness, the Lord whispered, *It's time to write.*

You see, God is stronger and a vital, passionate relationship with Him is the only means by which you and I will become stronger. I am absolutely sure God wanted me to write from a place of complete dependence on His truth, His Word, and His strength. He wanted you to know His strength, not mine. All those months I sat by Mama's bed and asked God to show me how He is stronger. Over and over, He did. I pray this study accurately reflects the truth of the only One who has the power make you stronger than the struggle you face today.

May the Lord be glorified in the lessons of my weakness. May His strength be evident to all. May He use these pages to transform our lives. Oh, how I pray that you see Him. Know Him. Love Him. Worship Him. I wish you could know how much I love you and pray for you all. I am honored to study the Scriptures alongside you.

By His strength, for His glory,
Angela

GOD IS STRONGER THAN EVERYTHING

Welcome, sweet friend. I am both humbled and honored to begin this first week of study with you. After months of research and more than a year of prayer for this message, it is with great joy that I share this profoundly simple truth: God is stronger than everything.

I have no idea what struggles you are bringing to our weeks of study, but I do know one powerful thing: whatever you are facing, the Bible promises our God is stronger.

stronger than your greatest weakness
stronger than your deepest need
stronger than your past mistakes
stronger than your present stumblings
stronger than sickness, physical sufferings, and death
stronger than your doubts
stronger than your bad attitude
stronger than broken relationships
stronger than leaders, authorities, kings, and nations
stronger than loneliness and depression
stronger than anxiety and worry
stronger than sin
stronger than unforgiveness
stronger than anger, bitterness, and rage

God is stronger than everything. And everybody. And every circumstance. Oh hallelujah!

Well, shoot. I have already started to cry. Right here on the first page, with these first words, But there is no sadness in my tears; these are tears of comfort and hope. God is stronger than everything that concerns me and I am emotional because I'm so grateful. Grateful to belong to the One called Almighty. Strong Tower. Refuge. Protector. Redeemer. Grateful that no matter what else happens today, I belong to Him. He is stronger. I am safe in His care. And because of His enduring love, He keeps making me stronger for each new day.

Longing to know more about the strength of God, I have been studying His Word, observing others, examining my own heart, and seeking the wisdom of greater scholars. An observation I keep encountering among Christ followers is this: many followers of Jesus face the same struggles and trials as everyone—their bodies and minds grow weary—yet God is making them stronger on their journey.

Other followers of Jesus know about the strength of God, yet they do not live in His power. They make their journey without power, marked by long stays in miserable places.

Even though you and I may believe in the same God and trust the same Jesus as Savior, we are not all receiving the same fresh strength God offers for the soul. Too many of us are living powerless lives, feeling overcome, defeated, weary, and even downright mad.

Some Christ followers have never understood the great mercy and grace of God for His people and try to make life's journey without His presence or strength for their souls.

For each of us, the same truth applies: a biblical relationship with the God of Glory is the only way we will ever walk in strength on this earth.

So welcome, my friends, new and old. It's good to circle our chairs and pursue God together. Move toward Him. Lean in closer to His love and His Word and His strength. This week we begin with searching questions to build a beautiful, biblical foundation for our study together.

We will ask the Scriptures:

How do we know God is stronger than everything?

We will ask of the theological study:

How does an Almighty God make His people stronger?

How does the Bible instruct us to receive God's promised strength?

We will ask of ourselves:

What needs to change in me so that I live in the strength God promises to provide?

God is stronger than everything. And He can make you stronger.

Oh, let it be for all of us! Amen and amen.

DAY 1

GOD ALMIGHTY

In my travels, I've met many women who tell me, "Your Bible study was the first I ever did." Every time I hear those sweet words, I'm deeply humbled, and I whisper thanks to God for trusting me with her precious time. I've also learned through those meetings that I can't assume we all begin a study with the same understanding of the Bible or the same basic assumptions about faith.

We are a beautiful variety of women at different places and ages and with different needs and struggles. So I'm praying these weeks together will become spiritual food for each of us, from the first-time Bible study girls to those of you who do your daily Bible reading in the Hebrew and Greek. By the power of the Holy Spirit, God through His Word is able to make each one of us stronger.

In today's study we begin with the source of all strength—God Almighty. Some of you know Him well. His presence is as familiar to you as the shape of your hand. For others, today it's my privilege to introduce you to the Maker of heaven and earth. He is the One who has always loved you. Sees you. Smiles that you are here.

Let's start today in prayer.

God, I want to know You more. I want to learn and grow and understand Your powerful words. In so many ways, I desperately need to become stronger, so teach me about who You are and the strength You give. Bring Your light into my dark places. For these next pages, help me to focus on You. Just You, Lord. Amen.

If you're anything like me, you know how tempting it is to begin this study by talking about myself. My needs. My stumbles. My struggles. All the places I want to be stronger. Need to be stronger.

But if we start by talking about ourselves, we will quickly lose heart, giving up the hope of ever becoming stronger. We have to start with God, because it's His strength we need, not a million more hours to focus on ourselves.

And so, my sisters, I give you the Lord God Almighty. He is stronger than everything.

THE OMNI-NESS OF GOD

The enormity of God's strength is a concept that will not fit inside my head. Nowhere is my smallness more evident than when I try to consider the attributes of God and how great they are.

Take a minute to remember some of the characteristics you know about God. I'll get you started. Finish the sentence, God is . . .
Faithful, Loving

I bet you've written amazing words about the character of God like "powerful, compassionate, merciful, forgiving." Now go back and before each of your words, add the word *omni-*. That's our God. In all His attributes, He is omni.

> OMNI *is a Latin word that means "all," "in all ways," "in all things," "every," or "everywhere." When omni is added to the start of a word, then "all" modifies the word and expands the meaning.*

The Bible doesn't use the prefix *omni* to describe God. Theologians constructed the expanded omni-words to help convey the vastness of God's attributes from the Bible. Let's take a look at three of these expanded words: omnipresence, omniscience, and omnipotence.

GOD IS OMNIPRESENT

God is present at all times and in all places. Perhaps one of the most beautiful passages regarding God's omnipresence is found in Psalm 139.

Read those 24 verses and use this space to write the key phrases that describe where God is.

UBIQUITOUS means existing or being everywhere at the same time.

Now look at these next passages. See how God fills the heavens and no one can hide from Him?

> Am I a God at hand, declares the LORD, and not a God far away? Can a man hide himself in secret places so that I cannot see him? declares the LORD. Do I not fill heaven and earth? declares the LORD.
> Jeremiah 23:23-24

This question is too easy, but humor me. Where can you go to get away from God's presence?

The Bible says people worship other gods that don't even exist, but our God is near when we pray.

> For what great nation is there that has a god so near to it as the LORD our God is to us, whenever we call upon him?
> Deuteronomy 4:7

See how the theology of God as omnipresent unfolds when we study the Scriptures? A.W. Tozer says that few truths are so clearly taught in the Scripture as "the doctrine of divine omnipresence." He continues: "God is everywhere here, close to everything, next to everyone."[1]

Don't you love that? God is here with me this morning and with you as you read these words. No matter how you feel or even if you can't feel anything, God is not far. You are in the same room with God. His character and this truth will never change. Which reminds me, God's unchanging character is called His immutability.

Which is your first reaction to God's ubiquity?

    ☐ *Oh no, I can never escape Him.*

    ☐ *Oh yes, He'll never leave me.*

Whichever answer you chose, why might others choose the opposite answer?

IMMUTABILITY means God changes not in His essence. He changes not in His attributes. God changes not in His plans. God is unchanging in His promises.[2]

God said these words concerning His immutability:

I the Lord do not change.
Malachi 3:6

Draw something here on earth that seems unchangeable.

So what does the immutability and omnipresence of God mean for you today? What does God's omnipresence have to do with His strength or you becoming stronger?

Well, hang on, friend, because each of God's attributes has everything to do with His strength for us and to us.

I just have to stop for one second to tell you, I LOVE this! I love that God reveals big, OMNI, mind-boggling, glorifying truths about Himself in the Bible and then reaches down into our lives to graciously provide that same greatness to change us and our circumstances and prove to us over and over that He loves us.

God's omnipresence is part of His strength. Look at these amazing passages and see for yourself:

God is our refuge and strength, an ever-present help in trouble.
Psalm 46:1 (NIV)

The Lord is near to all who call on him, to all who call on him in truth.
Psalm 145:18 (NIV)

(Jesus said) "Surely I am with you always, to the very end of the age."
Matthew 28:20 (NIV)

God is ever-present, near, with us always. Does that truth give you comfort? A deeper peace? Think about this for a minute: God is stronger than everything and He is here. Wherever you are, He is too. He promises to be with you always.

How has God been present in unexpected places in your life?

How can God's omnipresence settle your heart today? Quiet your fears? Restore your trust?

As we end our first day of study about one amazingly big truth, will you close your eyes, focus your mind on the Lord, and let your soul rest in the presence of God? He is stronger than everything. And you don't have to be. Hallelujah and amen.

> *Oh, there is, in contemplating Christ, a balm for every wound; in musing on the Father, there is a quietus for every grief; and in the influence of the Holy Ghost, there is a balsam for every sore. Would you lose your sorrows? Would you drown your cares? Then go, plunge yourself in the Godhead's deepest sea; be lost in his immensity; and you shall come forth as from a couch of rest, refreshed and invigorated. I know nothing which can so comfort the soul; so calm the swelling billows of grief and sorrow; so speak peace to the winds of trial, as a devout musing upon the subject of the Godhead.[3] —C. H. Spurgeon*

A LITTLE STRONGER—God is always with me. His strength is ever-present, in every place, for every circumstance I face.

DAY 2

GOD ALL-KNOWING AND ALL-POWERFUL

Last night I slept the sweetest sleep. Most of the day had been spent writing and praying through our lesson about God's presence. Before I turned off the light, I studied today's topic for a while then closed my eyes with God's words on my heart.

When I lay my head on my pillow and snuggled under the covers, it truly felt like I was tucking my physical body and all the worries of my day underneath the wings of God. The Almighty One. Our God who is *omni* in all His ways. Our refuge and strength and hope.

With one day focused entirely on the truth of God's presence, I slept like a baby without a care in the world. My soul had been reminded that God is standing guard. He is stronger than everything. And when your heart trusts God's truth, He gives a peace that replaces fears and worries with rest.

GOD IS OMNISCIENT

God knows everything. He is perfect in knowledge. His understanding is infinite. With all my heart, I hope and pray the truths of this study will give your soul rest.

We are going to spend one more day focused on the great strength of God. Goodness, we could spend years and maybe we should, but for now, let's jump into the next *omni* attribute of our Lord.

Father, focus my thoughts again today, so I can take in as much understanding as I am able. Increase my knowledge of You. Show me according to Your Word how strong and mighty You are. Amen.

With each of God's attributes, we encounter another great, big, *omni*-sized trait and this characteristic is no different. To consider God's vast, all-encompassing knowledge is once again more truth than our minds can conceive. But we are not alone; when the apostle Paul wrote his letter to the Romans, he echoed something similar:

> *Oh, the depth of the riches and wisdom and knowledge of God! How unsearchable are his judgments and how inscrutable his ways!*
> *Romans 11:33*

The knowledge of God is too much for us to fathom, yet it's important for us to examine. God's knowledge is one more facet of His strength.

The Bible is full of verses that refer to God's infinite knowledge. Let's read a few of these together (see sidebar).

How often have you wondered if God knows what's going on in your life? Your heart? Does He see what happens in your family? Can He have any idea about the struggles you face? Tell me your thoughts.

He does. The Bible affirms over and over that God knows everything.

Theologian Wayne Grudem defines God's omniscience like this: "God fully knows himself and all things actual and possible in one simple and external act."[4] That means He knows Himself and each one of us perfectly. He knows everything about you and me. All things—past, present, and future—and our secrets and our potential.

I love A.W. Tozer's writings so much. He wanted to make sure we did not have any questions left about the scope of God's knowledge when he wrote this:

> God knows instantly and effortlessly all matter and all matters, all mind and every mind, all spirit and all spirits, all being and every being, all creaturehood and all creatures, every plurality and all pluralities, all law and every law, all relations, all causes, all thoughts, all mysteries, all enigmas, all feeling, all desires, every unuttered secret, all thrones and dominions, all personalities, all things visible and invisible in heaven and in earth, motion, space, time, life, death, good, evil, heaven, and hell.[5]

Talk no more so very proudly, let not arrogance come from your mouth; for the LORD is a God of knowledge, and by him actions are weighed.
1 Samuel 2:3

For he looks to the ends of the earth and sees everything under the heavens.
Job 28:24

Do you know the balancings of the clouds, the wondrous works of him who is perfect in knowledge?
Job 37:16

Great is our Lord, and abundant in power; his understanding is beyond measure.
Psalm 147:5

For as the heavens are higher than the earth, so are my ways higher than your ways and my thoughts than your thoughts.
Isaiah 55:9

For whenever our heart condemns us, God is greater than our heart, and he knows everything.
1 John 3:20

Take a few minutes to look up some of these verses. It's so much better when we see God's truth for ourselves. Beside each passage, jot down what the verse says God knows.

Bible Passage	God Knows
Exodus 3:7	
1 Chronicles 28:9	
Proverbs 5:21	
Proverbs 15:3	
Matthew 6:30-32	
Matthew 10:30	

Based on everything we just read about the knowledge of God, answer these two questions:

How does the omniscience of God give you comfort?

How does that truth make you tremble?

GOD IS OMNIPOTENT

God has infinite power. He is Almighty. God can do everything.

This afternoon I think I have read every Bible verse that mentions the power of God. I wish we had time to read all those passages because it'll do something for you. My soul is full. My mind is excited. I just want to grab the next person down my street and sit her down to hear all the power verses. I want to holler from my front door, "Hey, buddy! The God you have been ignoring, well, He really is almighty. And here's the kicker—the Almighty still loves you."

> *It is a mighty conception that we form of a power from which all other power is derived . . . which nothing can oppose. . . . The omnipotence of God is inconceivable and boundless. It arises from the infinite perfection of God, that his power can never be actually exhausted.*[6] *—Richard Watson*

I'm praying these three verses will give you the big idea about God's power:

> *I know that You can do anything*
> *and no plan of Yours can be thwarted.*
> *Job 42:2 (HCSB)*

> *Jesus looked at them and said, "With man this is impossible, but with God all things are possible."*
> *Matthew 19:26*

> *For His invisible attributes, that is, His eternal power and divine nature, have been clearly seen since the creation of the world, being understood through what He has made. As a result, people are without excuse.*
> *Romans 1:20 (HCSB)*

These never-changing, glorious characteristics of God's nature—one on top of the other, all woven together—become proof that God is stronger than everything. He is stronger than any battle you will ever face. He is the source of all the strength you will ever need. From His never-changing *omni*-strength, God promises to be our strength, to give His strength to us, and—oh, thank goodness—to never tire of making us stronger. Not only is God omnipresent, omniscient, and omnipotent, the Bible goes on to say He is

invisible	personal	living	self-existent	eternal
unchanging	faithful	wise	loving	long-suffering
compassionate	free	sovereign	incomprehensible	holy
righteous	true	good	merciful	forgiving

Look at the list of characteristics and use these words to write a note for someone who comes to mind. What would you remind him or her about the nature of God?

My mama went to heaven two weeks ago today, so I'm writing my note to my daddy:

Sweet Daddy, God is wise. He is compassionate and merciful. He is unchanging and good. He loves you and will be faithful to you. He is with you now and is powerful enough to heal your heart. I trust Him for us all. I love you so much, but even better, God loves you perfectly.

To whom will you write a note about the truths of God?

To someone who's been praying for a great need?

To someone whose life is full of responsibilities and worries?

To someone who doesn't know Christ?

To yourself?

Well may the saint trust such a God! He is worthy of implicit confidence. Nothing is too hard for Him. If God were stinted in might and had a limit to His strength we might well despair. But seeing that He is clothed with omnipotence, no prayer is too hard for Him to answer, no need too great for Him to supply, no passion too strong for Him to subdue; no temptation too powerful for Him to deliver from, no misery too deep for Him to relieve.[7] *—Arthur Pink*

A LITTLE STRONGER—My God is almighty, all-knowing, and unchanging. He knows what I need even before I ask. Nothing is impossible for Him.

BELIEVING GOD LOVES YOU

Christian counselors are my heroes. I have been to several through the years and know many more. Every one I've ever met is amazing. Wise. Gracious. Understanding. Merciful. And patient, oh so very patient.

My counselor friends might spend months with clients, listening, instructing, and gently guiding them to apply biblical truths in their lives. Sometimes I wish God had given me the personality of a patient counselor, but I'm afraid I probably lean a little more toward drill sergeant. Smiling drill sergeant.

DRILL SERGEANT *[In the nicest possible way. Think capri pants, wedge sandals, and shiny pink lip gloss]—a noncommissioned officer who trains soldiers in basic military skills.*

The idea of Bible teacher/drill sergeant may not be a flattering picture of myself, especially if you've ever served in the military. But a part of me does want to call in the troops (all my girlfriends who follow Jesus), get us lined up (after oohing over everybody's cute shoes), outline our assignment (to live this life according to God's Word and for His glory), take a few questions, then holler, "All together now. Forward march!" I just want to see us all moving toward God, learning and growing together.

When I introduce a life-changing truth to a person in great need, my inner drill sergeant almost starts yelling for pure joy. "Over here! This is it! Right in front of us is the power to change everything! So, all together now, let's pick up this big truth and apply it to our lives. Steady on. Forward, ho. Let's keep walking with that truth. This. Is. So. Exciting!"

From the very first day God called me to teach the Bible, I have felt exactly this way. So full of joy over God's truth that sometimes I just want to yell or blow a whistle to get people's attention. The freshly minted seminary grad didn't know it, but now I do: not everyone gets as excited about truth. My passion is not their passion. My enthusiasm and research and convincing arguments are not motivating to them. Some people can hear life-changing truth for years, never do one thing about it, and then wonder why they keep fighting the same battles. Making the same mistakes. Hurting the same people.

Then there are people in great need who decide to become great at being needy. It's easier to stay needy than take hold of the power to change. They'd rather come back another time or talk about it later.

My passion wants to holler, "You want to talk about it? Think about it? Come back later? But this is it! Here is the place where your whole life changes. Why are you turning away when the answer is here?"

Can you tell I have a fire in my bones about this subject? And in case you and I only met two days ago, I do want you to know I only yell when my boy scores in soccer. I do realize not one person has ever been yelled into believing God. So I keep the yelling inside, but my heart still pleads, *Please don't waste one more day just looking at God's truth. Let's live this.*

Our first two days, I did my best to cram into these little pages a review of God's character. The Bible is convincing.

> *The sum of God's attributes = God's awesome strength.*

He is the source of strength for all who follow Him. That is don't-miss-this kind of truth. Sometimes when people learn about the greatness of God, they commit the rest of their lives to following Him. But I've also watched too many people walk away.

Do you know why many turn away from an awesome God? They cannot believe God loves them enough.

They feel unworthy to receive His strength. Undeserving. Ashamed.

But there is no "enough" for us with God. Good enough. Kind enough. Generous enough. We do not earn His love because we have finally become enough. We are not disqualified from His love because we could never be enough.

AGAPE LOVE *—a self-giving love that seeks the highest good in the one loved, no matter how unworthy that person may be.*

To believe God loves you is crucial to our journey in this life. In this study, we are moving toward God. To stay in unbelief makes you a straggler, and I'm just not willing to leave you behind. You have to understand God to know you are truly loved by God.

What you believe about God's love will make all the difference. Don't listen to hearsay and rumors. Study. Search. Learn about His love.

What comes into our minds when we think about God is the most important thing about us.[8] —*A.W. Tozer*

How would you explain to a new believer what Tozer was saying?

LOVED BY GOD

We will never comprehend all of God's nature, but we can embrace all the revelation given to us in His Word. To believe God cannot love you enough is to completely miss the truth of God's revealed character.

God freely gives His love to all. In case you thought otherwise, none of us could be enough anyway. Not me. Not you. Not even the cute woman in your group with a tote bag full of underlined Bibles. We're sinners—all of us. Yet God graciously loves each one of us.

> *For while we were still weak, at the right time Christ died for the ungodly. For one will scarcely die for a righteous person—though perhaps for a good person one would dare even to die—but God shows his love for us in that while we were still sinners, Christ died for us.*
> *Romans 5:6-8*

From the verses above, answer the following.
What state were we in when Christ died for us?

For whom did Christ die?

Finish this sentence: "God shows His love for us in that . . .

Just to clarify one more time: Jesus Christ came and died because God wanted to show His love for weak, ungodly sinners. I'm pretty sure that includes all of us. I guess I've said it a thousand times, but it bears repeating here. You do not send your Only Son for the ones you like just a little. You send your Only Son because of love.

ARE YOU LIMITING GOD?
Not believing God could love you enough is, in essence, like taking a swipe at His glory.

Have you ever heard anyone say things like these?

- My sins are too many to be forgiven.
- I believe God can forgive me; I just don't think He's willing.
- My heart is hard and I don't feel God's love.
- My sin is too ugly.
- I've been this way too long.
- I keep making the same mistakes over and over.
- I read about the promises of God's love, but He does not mean me.

I understand how these thoughts get into our heads. We've all been tempted to let our minds go there. Satan is a liar who speaks lies to us that seem right and justified, so we believe him.

We look at ourselves and take inventory of our lives and agree with him. *Yep, my sin is too big and my heart is too hard and I'm too far gone. God could never love me enough to help me now.* And Satan smiles because he wins. You and I remain powerless, moping through this life apart from the love of God, focused on ourselves and our sin and our never-ending mess. Sad, then angry, and one day, full of despair.

How is the idea that you are unique in your sin an expression of misguided pride?

Here is the deal. To embrace the lies of Satan is to elevate your sin above the grace of God. You are saying to God, *My sin has more power than Your omnipotence.* You are limiting the blood of Jesus, shed to wash away the sins of the world . . . but not yours. You are limiting the love of God, great enough to deliver a nation of backsliders, big enough to forgive a murderer named Paul, but just short of big enough for you.

I beg you, do not limit the love of God. Do not limit His long-suffering—He has not run out of patience.

- Do not limit His grace—He can melt the hardest of hearts.
- Do not limit His power—He is not thwarted by "been this way too long."
- Do not limit His faithfulness—He is with you always.
- Do not limit His methods—He does as He wills, and in all His ways, He is loving.
- Do not limit His promises—what He has said, He will do.
- Do not limit the work of His Son on the cross—Jesus' death has the power to save all.
- Do not limit His forgiveness—He forgives even the vilest of sin.
- Do not limit His joy—He still has plans for your good.

If you haven't already, are you now willing to believe in God's love? Will you turn your focus from the lies and toward the glorious truth of God's Word? To believe God is a decision that changes everything.

When you have chosen to believe, then you are ready to begin living this life in a relationship with the One who is eternally in love with you.

Why don't you take a minute to tell God you believe He loves you. Write your thoughts.

Do you know what happens when I tell God I believe that He loves me? I cry. Every single time. But I cry because I'm grateful. So very grateful He would love an ol' sinner like me.

He has always loved me. He has always loved you.

10 WAYS TO BE DELIBERATE IN PURSUING THE CLOSENESS OF GOD

1. Call upon Him.
   Jeremiah 29:12
2. Seek Him with your whole heart.
   Jeremiah 29:13
3. Love Him.
   Proverbs 8:17
4. Wait for Him.
   Lamentations 3:25
5. Ask Him anything.
   Matthew 7:7-8
6. Have faith in Him.
   Hebrews 11:6
7. Trust Him.
   Psalm 9:10
8. Do everything in His name.
   Colossians 3:17
9. Praise Him.
   Hebrews 13:15
10. Return to Him.
    Isaiah 55:6-7

Keep yourselves in the love of God.
Jude 21

Millions of people, both inside and outside the church, believe that the essential message of Christianity is, "If you behave, then you belong." From a human standpoint, that's why most people reject Christianity. A friend of mine told me the other day that the reason his now-deceased father never went to church was that he didn't think he was good enough. He said his dad thought church was all about a good person telling other good people how to be better people. But that's not what the Bible says.[9] —Tullian Tchividjian

A LITTLE STRONGER—God's love for me is stronger than my understanding. Stronger than my failings. Stronger than my feelings. I will not limit the love of God.

NEAR TO GOD

"Oh my," followed by "Whew!" were the brilliant words mumbled by the last person who came into my study. I smiled and told her, "Just try not to look."

Like every person who's opened my door the past couple of months, she looked like she wanted to faint or run. There are stacks of sorted notes, piles of books, and different colored stickies everywhere. All this craziness makes my friends nervous because they want to straighten, but it's my little world. I'm in my happy place, studying and sorting and working at understanding God's Word.

> *An impactful [study] requires a solid foundation of truth, or it will crumble under its own weight.*[10] *—Charles Swindoll*

When it comes to Bible study, God made me for logic. Sometimes, I begin with emotion or intuition about a subject, but never feel good about my approach until I have discovered the biblical framework on which to build.

I usually launch like a rocket, ordering ten books too many and going overboard with my fancy Logos Bible study software. But eventually, from the piles of notes and journals and stickies and prayers, the way toward God's truth becomes clear.

The ability to study and understand the Word of God is available to all of us—small town mamas or big city girls. Each one of us can open the Bible, read, study, pray, and learn. Our God is faithful and true. He is not playing games with us or changing His mind. He loves us. Jesus died for us. The Bible speaks to us. The Holy Spirit works in us. And in all these things, God is glorified.

Several months ago, I jotted a note to myself, "How does one receive the strength of God?"

With no worrying about right or wrong answers, how would you respond to that question?

My first thought was, "You just ask. Ask God for the strength you need." While that answer isn't wrong, the next question becomes, "Then why aren't more of us living stronger lives if all we have to do is ask?"

So I had to dig. And sort. And observe. And pray. I believe the Bible has constructed a logical path for us. This week's study is my understanding about the steps any of us can take to receive the strength of God.

Yes, you and I are instructed to ask for God's strength. But before we can ask in faith, we have to understand who we are asking and why He is both willing and able to supply strength. Some may know God is Almighty, but still don't ask for His strength because they cannot believe God loves them enough.

And maybe some ask for God's strength, but they are far off. In the Bible, God gives His strength to those who have come near.

Today, are you near to God or far away?

We can whine and pout and stomp over wanting to be made stronger. We can quote a Bible verse and say nice things about the Almighty, but God does not give His strength from a distance.

Could it be that your life without strength is a reflection of where you are with God? I have never seen God hurl His strength out to someone with her back turned to Him. Or give strength to someone who lives far away from Him. God gives His strength to those close by—to the one who has turned toward Him and has run back into His presence.

> *Draw near to God, and he will draw near to you.*
> *James 4:8*

INTO HIS PRESENCE
Turn in your Bible to Mark 2:1-12. Three of the Gospels record this story, but Mark gives us more details, so we'll settle in here for a few minutes.

1. What obstacles stood between the paralyzed man and Jesus?

2. What caused Jesus to give the power of His forgiveness?

3. What happened when Jesus made the weak man with great faith stronger (v.12)?

You probably remember this account from a childhood Sunday School lesson. A paralyzed man's friends bring him to see Jesus. The home where Jesus is teaching is so full, the man cannot get in. There isn't even room to stand near the door. So the four friends of the paralyzed man carry him up what were probably outside stairs to the roof. Then they dug a hole through the roof, large enough to lower the man down on his bed.

Many of the background details are missing, but what we know for sure is four men worked hard to get their paralyzed friend into the presence of Jesus. We don't know who was directing the project. Maybe it was one of the friends, but I truly believe the man who needed the Lord was doing all the talking:

Will you take me to Jesus? They say He's in a home over there.
What do you mean, it's standing room only? Then take me right up to the door.
There's no room at the door? Then take me onto the roof.
OK, now dig a hole! Bigger. Big enough for me and my bed. I have to get to Him.
OK, good, now everybody grab a corner and lower me down. Don't worry about me. I'll hang on; just get me in front of that man.

I believe this man had heard about the powerful presence of Jesus. He'd heard about Jesus' power to forgive, restore life, and heal. He determined in his heart to get to the only one with that kind of strength. He had to get into Jesus' presence.

As the story unfolds, when Jesus saw their faith, the man's sins were forgiven and he was healed. Then, at Jesus' instruction, the man stood up, picked up his bed, and walked home.

This paralyzed man was not healed at his home, far away from the Lord. By faith, he earnestly sought and received power in the presence of Jesus. And there, in the presence of Jesus, he was made stronger.

So I ask, do you want Jesus to make you stronger? We cannot keep asking for His strength from a distance. Go to Him. Do whatever you have to do to be where He is.

- Ask someone to show you the way.
- Ask people to carry you if you must.
- Determine that nothing will keep you from knowing the closeness of God.
- Draw near to God so that your spirit, emotions and physical body can be made stronger.

> *We never grow closer to God when we just live life; it takes deliberate pursuit and attentiveness.*[11] *—Francis Chan*

What are the characteristics of a life lived close to God?

Maybe you have discovered these for yourself, or maybe you know a person who lives in God's presence.

What kind of strength does God give to those who stay near Him?

The Lord does not force us into a close relationship with Him. He's too good for that. He reveals His lavish love and then allows us to choose.

In Luke 15, the father watched as his prodigal son chose to take his inheritance and move to a distant country. While his son was away squandering his life, the father never stopped loving him, but apart from his father, the son suffered all the consequences of his sin and his choices. Only when the prodigal returned did he encounter the grace of his father for his mistakes.

> For you were straying like sheep, but have now returned to the Shepherd and Overseer of your souls.
> 1 Peter 2:25

God isn't angry at His people and won't be angry at anyone who comes to Him. Our sin is big but God's grace is bigger. It's okay to trust God because He never makes mistakes. You can laugh and sing and be free, because the Son makes you free. You don't become faithful in order to get loved and get free—you are already free and loved and that is why it's possible to be faithful. —Steve Brown[12]

And so, my friend, why don't we stay? Stay close to God. Stay close to His forgiveness, His grace, and His love. Stay close to His strength and the power to change. And today, if you have been far off, hear the Father calling your name: "Hey, _____. Stay close to Me. I am your strength."

A LITTLE STRONGER—I will never become stronger far away from God. His strength is transferred to those who are close. Oh Father, by Your strength, keep me close.

SURRENDER

Today is a really important day for this study, so call your girlfriend and tell her, "If you can complete only one day this week, make sure you do Day 5!" I've been praying for all of you and I'm so glad we are working through the truths together. My soul is thirsty for God, so let's begin.

Let's review the question that set this Bible study in motion:

If God is stronger than everything, and He is, then why do so many believers still live in tragic weakness?

The past four days, we've seen several truths about God's strength according to the Bible.

- God is almighty in all His ways.
- God is stronger than everything and completely able to make you stronger.
- God has proven His enduring love for you over and over.
- God calls you close to Him where His strength is given.

The logical next question is, *Will you choose to receive His strength?*

Will you surrender your personal plan for becoming stronger and accept God's plan, God's terms, God's methods, and God's ways?

I'm writing to you a little brokenhearted, thinking of people I love very much who live this tragedy everyday. I call it a tragedy because when people keep refusing the grace of God, they face a desperate, repetitive sadness. *Aren't you tired yet?* I wonder.

But quick as lightening, the Holy Spirit prompts me: *Angela, search yourself. Where are you lacking surrender? Where are you still seeking your own strength? Focused on your meticulous plans? Your version of how your life should go? Your children's lives? Your ministry? Preoccupied with your fear, your weakness, your insecurity? Aren't you tired yet?*

Then comes the kind voice of my Father: *Baby girl, I AM able to make you STRONGER.*

I'm praying the Holy Spirit will remind our moping, self-focused, defeated selves of something important: because of the great love of God, Jesus has already bought our strength on the cross. It's done. He is stronger. He is Lord. And He is glorified when you respond with your life. Stop trying to be your own strength. He is the only one who can make you stronger.

This walk with God toward strength runs completely opposite of everything they taught in my business classes. There they encouraged us to do the following:

- Make a plan, work the plan, then receive the benefits.
- Follow the rules and eventually there will be a payoff.

Maybe you've been taught similar things. We can earn many things in this world by strategy and wit, but we can never earn what God intends to give us for free.

Jesus already bought our strength with His life. He offers it to us as a gift of grace. And as a gift, it is something you cannot earn, so it's time for Christ-followers to stop making up rules restricting the gift. No rules govern how worthy we are to receive His strength and no rules can manipulate the mind of God. When people receive strength from God, they receive it on God's terms, not their own merit. They can never keep enough rules to make it happen.

From the Scriptures, maybe the following steps could become our working theology for becoming stronger.

Beside each of these four steps, write a word or two to remind yourself of a time when you took that particular step.

1. Believe

2. Ask

3. Surrender

4. Receive

We are studying what it means to receive God's strength because those four simple words I just typed come with many challenges. The purpose of these weeks is to face those challenges according to Scripture, so that, with God's help, we can live in greater victory—stronger.

I have been with people who are suffering desperately. I prayed, they prayed, and hundreds prayed for them. But new strength never seemed to be given.

What about you? Have you prayed for strength that seemingly did not come?

It would be easy to think God overlooked our prayers, allowing anger and bitterness into our hearts—not the strength to endure for which we had all prayed. I've had times when I wondered if God had decided not to give His strength—an idea that runs counter to everything the Bible teaches:

> *God is our refuge and strength, a very present help in trouble.*
> *Psalm 46:1*

God is not *sometimes* our strength. He is *at all times* a very present help.

> *After you have suffered a little while, the God of all grace, who has called you to his eternal glory in Christ, will himself restore, confirm, strengthen, and establish you.*
> *1 Peter 5:10*

God promises that He will strengthen us in our suffering.

> *But he said to me, "My grace is sufficient for you, for my power is made perfect in weakness." Therefore I will boast all the more gladly of my weaknesses, so that the power of Christ may rest upon me.*
> *2 Corinthians 12:9*

The apostle Paul says that in great weakness, the power of Christ rests on us. God does not withhold His strengthening power when we are weak.

I can do all things through him who gives me strength.
Philippians 4:13 (NIV)

In the above passage, I understand the word "all" to mean "all." In all types of suffering and struggle and heartache, Christ promises to give us strength. I just can't find any instance in the Bible where God refused to give His strength to one who believed He was God and asked by faith.

After much observation and prayer, I have concluded that God always gives what He has promised, but sometimes we refuse the strength God provides.

Do you think that statement could be true? How might we refuse the strength God provides?

We want and need God's strength, but we want it on our terms. In the way we envisioned. With the outcome we desired. According to our purpose and our plan.

When we abandon the truth of God, we also abandon hope and the strength God has given to face our circumstances.

Can you think of any biblical examples of believers wanting God's strength only on their own terms?

I thought about some of the early followers of Jesus who wanted Him to be the Messiah but only on their own terms. They wanted a military leader to free them from Roman bondage. Maybe that's part of why they so quickly turned against Him.

Receiving God's strength means we choose to surrender to His wisdom. His timing. His greater purpose. His mystery. We have to trust Him to surrender to Him.

Trust is not a passive state of mind. It is a vigorous act of the soul by which we choose to lay hold on the promises of God and cling to them despite the adversity that at times seeks to overwhelm us.[13] —Jerry Bridges

Surrendering means that we trust in the following:

- God's sovereignty and timing for our lives
- God's method of giving us what we need
- God's provision from the fullness of His love
- God's heart being good and unchanging

Maybe those who refuse the strength of God hope they can direct the mind of God with their prayers. But Daniel says this about the Lord:

> He does as according to his will among the host of heaven and among the inhabitants of the earth.
> Daniel 4:35

Will you and I learn to trust God so completely that we intentionally, in all things, surrender our will to His?

If we are going to mature as Christ followers, then we must undertake this work of surrender—learning to give up how we thought it had to be, trusting the Lord God Almighty who gave us breath—so that every obstacle is removed and we are able to receive His promised strength.

> *[It] often seems more difficult to trust God than to obey Him. . . . The circumstances in which we must trust God often appear irrational and unreasonable. . . . Obeying God is worked out within well-defined boundaries of God's revealed will. But trusting God is worked out in an arena that has no boundaries.[14] —Jerry Bridges*

Learning to believe, ask, surrender, and receive the strength of God has a purpose: so God will be glorified. Before we finish this day, take a minute to complete the following:

My _____ + God's strength = God's glory.

Circle any words you could use to fill in the blank above.

weakness	needs	sickness	timidity	deficits
shortcomings	cowardliness	fears	failings	imperfection
inadequacy	indecision	powerlessness	lack	poverty
exhaustion	meekness	grief	persecution	struggles
emptiness	mistakes	addiction	wounds	

Now look at the circled words and pray through each one:

God, glorify Yourself in my _____.

A LITTLE STRONGER—I will trust the Lord in all His ways. I will not refuse His strength nor will I diminish His glory.

VIEWER GUIDE SESSION 2

PSALM 84

BLESSED ARE THOSE WHOSE STRENGTH IS IN HIM

Psalm 84:1-4

Pilgrim Psalms

Psalm 84:5-12

1. The psalmist is on a _____ to the _____.

2. It points to the _____ Who is _____.

3. We are given a _____ of what it is like to live this life on _____ as Christians.

Either you are walking toward eternity _____ _____ or you are walking toward eternity _____ _____.

How will I be one of the blessed whose strength is in God?

Colossians 2:9

Colossians 2:13-15

Colossians 3:11

John 15:5—"You can do _____ without Me" (HCSB).

WEEK 2

GOD IS STRONGER THAN MY STRUGGLES

We are living in an isolation that would have been unimaginable to our ancestors, and yet we have never been more accessible. Within this world of instant and absolute communication, unbounded by limits of time or space, we suffer from unprecedented alienation. We have never been more detached from one another, or lonelier. In a world consumed by ever more novel modes of socializing, we have less and less actual society . . . Facebook arrived in the middle of a dramatic increase in the quantity and intensity of human loneliness, a rise that initially made the site's promise of greater connection seem deeply attractive . . . [yet] Americans are more solitary than ever before.[2]

WITH LONELINESS

"Turn to me and be gracious to me,
for I am lonely and afflicted."
    —King David, between 1010 and 970 BC

"I'm so lonesome I could cry."
    —Hank Williams, 1949

Headlines report loneliness has become an epidemic, but you probably didn't need a headline to tell you. Many of our hearts have already encountered the same pain. Professional researchers say our culture has become the most disconnected, socially isolated, loneliest community of people ever.[1] I can't speak from years of research, but most of the people I know would agree: we are such a lonely bunch. Another psalmist wrote:

I am like a desert owl of the wilderness, like an owl of the waste places; I lie awake; I am like a lonely sparrow on the housetop.
Psalm 102:6-7

Ever known what it feels like to be the desert owl in the wilderness? To lie awake through the night? To go through the motions of one more day, lonely as a sparrow on the rooftop? I have. I bet you have too.

The reasons for our loneliness are as diverse as our personalities and journeys. I knew great loneliness in my single mom years. Often the pain was excruciating and paralyzing. I'm watching my dad suffer the loneliness of my mom's death. They spent fifty-one years together. How could you not be lonely after your best friend goes to heaven? Some of our friends are college students and lonely. Married and lonely. Single and lonely. Without children and lonely. Fighting disease and lonely. Oh my, how wide this struggle reaches.

Remember your loneliest time? What details made it particularly difficult?

Ever tried to cure your loneliness? Marriage. Children. A puppy. A hobby. Some of us find a cure for loneliness, but then it circles back around to us another way. Coming to terms with this struggle for myself has meant finally understanding lonely times are just going to occur on this journey. Read the following words from Charles Spurgeon:

> No Believer traverses all the road to heaven in company. There must be lonely spots here and there, though the greater part of our heavenward pilgrimage is made cheerful by the society of fellow travelers.

> Christ's sheep love to go in flocks. We take sweet counsel together and walk to the House of God in company. Yet somewhere or other on the road, every Christian will find narrow paths and close places where pilgrims must march in single file.[3]

Don't you love this vivid description? At times we will walk single file, while still in the company of believers. Believers in front. Believers behind. All going home to be with the Lord. That's the kind of loneliness we can experience as believers, but can you imagine loneliness apart from Jesus? I shudder at the thought of such a desperate place.

For the Christian, God is stronger than any loneliness we will ever face. From His strength, God made a promise to us.

I will never leave you nor forsake you.
Hebrews 13:5

Greek scholars tell us that our English Bibles don't translate the full weight of this verse. Rewritten with the force the original language intended, it goes like this:

The promise and guarantee in Hebrews 13:5 was spoken by God Himself. The word "leave" is not the usual word which means, "to leave," *leipo* (λειπο), but *aniemi* (ἀνιεμι) "to send back, to relax, to loosen, not to uphold, to let sink." It is preceded by two negatives in the Greek text, which in English make a positive, but which in Greek only serve to strengthen the negation. It is "I will not, I will not cease to sustain and uphold thee."

The word "forsake" is a compound of three Greek words, *egkataleipo, eg* (ἐγκαταλειπο, ἐγ) meaning "in," *kata* (κατα) meaning "down," and *leipo* (λειπο) meaning "to leave." *Leipo* (Λειπο) has the idea of forsaking one, *kata* (κατα) suggests rejection, defeat, helplessness, and *eg* (ἐγ) refers to some place or circumstance in which a person may find himself helpless and forsaken. The meaning of the word is that of forsaking someone in a state of defeat or helplessness in the midst of hostile circumstances. The word in its totality means "to abandon, desert, leave in straits, leave helpless, leave destitute, leave in the lurch, let one down." There are three negatives before this word, making the promise one of triple assurance: "I will not, I will not, I will not let thee down, leave thee in the lurch, leave thee destitute, leave thee in straits and helpless, abandon thee."[4]

Mamertine Prison—Rome, Italy

While researching the prison from which Paul wrote 2 Timothy, I read about the Mamertine prison located near the Forum in Rome and almost skipped a breath. I've been there. While chaperoning a school trip with my daughter's class, this prison was one of our stops.

Most believe Paul's second imprisonment was here. Tradition suggests that Peter also spent time in the same facility.

The cell is a gloomy, underground, cave-type room. We went down stairs that did not originally exist. Paul would have been thrown down into the cell from a hole above. The memory of that cell is vivid. The dim lights. Low ceilings. Everything was damp and cold.

Paul's loneliness is all the more understandable to me. I only stood for a few uncomfortable minutes in what must have been a miserable and awful place.

I will not, I will not, I will not let you down, leave you in a lurch, leave you destitute, leave you in straits or helpless, or abandon you.

God speaks to us here with layered, elaborate language to reaffirm and guarantee His promise. The believer will have His gracious presence in life, at death, and forever. We may struggle with times of loneliness, but this promise always holds, as we're lonely but never forsaken by God.

A LONELY APOSTLE

The apostle Paul wrote many of his letters from the loneliness of a prison cell. In those ancient jails, there were no modern-day cures for his loneliness, but as a follower of Jesus, Paul had what he needed, the promise of God's faithfulness.

Today, I want us to look at one of the passages Paul wrote while in the Mamertine prison in Rome. Turn to 2 Timothy 4:9-22.

Paul was probably about seventy-one when he wrote his second letter to Timothy. From the tone of his writing, Paul seems to know this would be the last letter he'd write to his friend. The letter teaches us much about a believer struggling with loneliness. Paul had multiple reasons to be lonely:

1. His living conditions were unpleasant—he was imprisoned in Rome (1:8,16-17).
2. Winter was approaching (4:21).
3. He'd been abandoned by his friends (4:10,14-16).
4. He missed his friend and ministry partner (4:9).
5. Death was close. For Paul, that would mean execution (4:6).

What correlation do you see between Paul's experience and places where you have struggled with loneliness?

Consider the second point above. Many people I know dread winter. Their loneliness increases with the darkness, the cold, and holiday celebrations.

Now look at some of the ways Paul chose to treat his loneliness. As you read, underline those healthy actions you can take.

- Paul asked for the visits of godly and trusted friends (4:9,11,21).
- He asked for physical comfort from the cold (4:13).
- He asked for his books to keep his mind occupied. These would not have been Scripture but additional teaching (4:13).
- He asked for "above all the parchments," which were probably his copies of the Old Testament (4:13).
- He genuinely forgave those who had abandoned him (4:16).
- He reaffirmed that his strength came from the never-forsaking presence of God (4:17).
- He kept his hope secure in Jesus Christ, his Savior (4:18).
- He kept his worship focused on the glory of God (4:18).
- He turned his thoughts away from himself and onto the welfare of his friends (4:19-22).

My sweet friends, this is just one passage. How rich is the Word of God for our everyday lives and struggles. Are you suffering with loneliness today? Maybe God has provided a remedy for you in the example of how Paul dealt with his loneliness.

Do you need to fortify yourself against the return of loneliness? Write about at least one action from Paul's list you can take.

Be strong and courageous. Do not fear or be in dread of them, for it is the LORD your God who goes with you. He will not leave you or forsake you.
Deuteronomy 31:6

Even though I walk through the valley of the shadow of death, I will fear no evil, for you are with me; your rod and your staff, they comfort me.
Psalm 23:4

LONELINESS

Genesis 2:18 assures us God is concerned about our loneliness. God encourages the lonely and takes care of lonely people (Ps. 68:6). The great commission assures us that God remains with us (Matt. 28:20). Life without God is a lonely existence, and we are particularly vulnerable when we are lonely (Eccles. 4:10-11).

The average American today probably meets as many people in one year as the average person did in a lifetime 100 years ago. Yet we're far lonelier. The presence of other people doesn't necessarily help loneliness at all.

Several recent surveys suggest that lonely people, especially teenagers, reach out through their social networks, desperately looking for someone who cares. We continue to crave personal interactions—perhaps more so because we have electronic witness to the interactions of others. Yet somehow, in a world where anyone can get attention online, we've moved away from authentic community. We Christians can see this as an opportunity to reach out to disenfranchised, lonely people and show the love of Christ, a man who knows sorrow and pain.

Paul's second letter to Timothy illustrates how feelings of loneliness are amplified by pain. He makes one of the most candid statements in the Bible:

At my first defense no one came to stand by me, but all deserted me. May it not be charged against them! But the Lord stood by me and strengthened me, so that through me the message might be fully proclaimed and all the Gentiles might hear it. So I was rescued from the lion's mouth. The Lord will rescue me from every evil deed and bring me safely into his heavenly kingdom. To him be the glory forever and ever. Amen.
2 Timothy 4:16-18

Paul is angry and hurt, but he's well aware that God has been and will continue to be his strength. He acknowledges that he needs and craves community, but he clearly states that God is foremost in his life.[5]

A Montana sheepherder wrote a strange request to a Chicago radio station. He lived a lonely life with his dog, four thousand sheep, a battery radio, and an old violin. He loved to listen to the symphony orchestra and wished he could play along with it in the parts that he knew.

Unfortunately, his violin was out of tune. He asked, "Some time before you start the next program, would you have the orchestra play A for me?"

Just before the next Chicago Symphony broadcast, thousands of listeners heard these words: "The orchestra will now play A for a sheepherder in Montana."[6]

> A LITTLE STRONGER—I may become lonely on my journey toward home, but I am not alone. God promised never to leave me. That truth makes all the difference. Even in loneliness, I will not despair; my hope is secure in my Savior.

WITH TEMPTATION

Welcome to Day Two of struggling, which would be a tad disheartening but for one great truth: God is stronger. So when you open this book and feel like the day's title just yelled at you, let your heart be filled with hope. God has not brought you to these pages to beat you up. He is not like that. When we turn to God with our struggles, He is merciful.

Thankfully we will not have to face all of life's struggles at the same time (whew and thank you, Jesus!). But be advised: very often yesterday's struggle with loneliness will sneak into our lives holding hands with temptation. At other times, temptation just waltzes in by itself. As we will learn today from the Scripture, in either case, our responsibility is to be alert.

This morning I woke up thinking about the broad spectrum of women who will do this Bible study. I've taught the Bible to women in the fellowship hall at my church; the side room at a country club; a highly guarded glass room at the women's prison; and just last week, under some trees in the rain. These diverse groups have taught me many truths; one being not to assume I know everyone's reality. The woman who sits beside you may dress like you and talk like you, but her journey is unique. Her struggles are not all the same as yours.

But here is the blessing for all: the Word of God will meet the needs of all.

Early in my ministry, I worried about not having something in common with the women I spoke to. I have learned to just teach the Bible. The Holy Spirit, by His power, uses the Scripture to make connections and work in all our hearts.

I won't ask you to stand up and share your recent struggle with temptation. (I don't believe the Lord is interested in another public round of Trump My Temptation.) But I do hope you'll spend this study becoming completely honest with yourself and with God. The Word of God is powerful when you allow its truth to go deep into your need.

Maybe you're being tempted to just skim through another Bible study. Maybe you already know all this stuff. But don't skim, my friend. Don't miss God's power again.

SATAN THE TEMPTER

It always goes back to him, doesn't it? Satan, the relentless deceiver, is still after you and me. He has not given up. He has not decreased his efforts. He has not marked you off as too old, too smart, too far gone, or too godly. He. Is. After. You. Mark it down.

Satan wants to exploit your weaknesses to keep you from living in obedience to God. Why? Because God supplies power for your life when you live in obedience. Satan wants you to stay in weakness, so he tempts without ceasing. He tempted Adam and Eve in the garden (Gen. 3:1-5), Jesus in the wilderness (Matt. 4:1-11), and followers of God (Josh. 7:21; 2 Sam. 11:2-4; Job 2:4-5; and Matt. 16:23, to name a few).

But Satan is not alone in his work. Even without him in the picture, we are still left with our sinful natures:

> *But each person is tempted when he is lured and enticed by his own desire.*
> *James 1:14*

And the other people in this world:

> *By appealing to the lustful desires of the flesh, they entice people who are just escaping from those who live in error.*
> *2 Peter 2:18 (NIV)*

Do not be mistaken because the Bible is clear: we will face temptation because of Satan, our own fallen nature, and the sin in this world, but God does not tempt us.

> *Let no one say when he is tempted, "I am being tempted by God," for God cannot be tempted with evil, and he himself tempts no one.*
> *James 1:13*

TEMPTED TO BELIEVE I'M NOT TEMPTED

Some of us are very aware of our weak places and the opportunities for temptation. What scares me more is those of us who've numbed our awareness of temptation. Is that you?

Maybe you're thinking to yourself, *Well, none of the biggies are tempting to me.*

- Cheat on my husband? No.
- Run a drug cartel? Nope.
- Steal from the makeup counter? Nay.
- Take revenge on my neighbor? Not so much.

You might think you're doing pretty well on the temptation thing. Then again, the Bible says temptation is common to man (1 Cor. 10:13). That's me and you and every Jesus-following girl in the room. We all struggle.

Let me get you thinking. Are you ever tempted to

- hold a grudge?
- share a confidence?
- make yourself and your problems the center of the world?
- withhold your love?
- withhold your forgiveness?
- turn your eyes away from the poor, the needy, the widow?
- gossip instead of pray?
- divide instead of unite people, church, and family?
- highlight the faults of the people you've been called to love?
- hide when God told you to go?
- judge instead of encourage?
- let a spirit of bitterness become your calling card?
- focus on your wants instead of your blessings?

Are you feeling a little anxious right now? I hope so, because I want the company! Oh how pitiful and embarrassing this is. Never let yourself think for a minute that you have somehow outgrown temptation.

Add three more temptations you struggle with.

1.

2.

3.

So here we are, each of us facing our own versions of temptation. No matter how subtle or brazen, each temptation leads us toward disobedience to Christ. But oh, hallelujah, God is stronger. Read Paul's promise to the Corinthians:

> No temptation has overtaken you that is not common to man. God is faithful, and he will not let you be tempted beyond your ability, but with the temptation he will also provide the way of escape, that you may be able to endure it.
> 1 Corinthians 10:13

Using the verse, fill in these blanks:

God is _____.

He will not let you be _____ _____ your ability.

He will also provide a _____ of _____.

Do you need more assurance God is committed to His promise? He will help you. Read these:

> For because he himself (Jesus) has suffered when tempted, he is able to help those who are being tempted.
> Hebrews 2:18

> The Lord knows how to rescue the godly from trials.
> 2 Peter 2:9

God promises to always do His part. He is faithful. He is able. He is our rescuer. He is stronger.

WE ARE NOT OVERTAKEN

On this journey home to God, one of the worst things we can do is think we're finally rising above common sin. In case you haven't noticed, Satan has no new tricks. He keeps on using the same old ones in the same old ways—common temptations in the lives of ordinary girls.

But here is the secret too many of us miss: the temptations you encounter—whether really big and awful or sneaky and tiny—do not have the power to overtake you. God has stepped in with His strength to keep you from falling.

How does a common woman with common temptations surrender to the strength God wants to provide? The Bible tells us how:

1. KEEP AWAKE SPIRITUALLY. BE WATCHFUL AND ALERT.

Be sober-minded; be watchful. Your adversary the devil prowls around like a roaring lion, seeking someone to devour.
1 Peter 5:8

Keep watch on yourself, lest you too be tempted.
Galatians 6:1

2. STAY CLOSE TO GOD.

For we do not have a high priest who is unable to sympathize with our weaknesses, but one who in every respect has been tempted as we are, yet without sin. Let us then with confidence draw near to the throne of grace, that we may receive mercy and find grace to help in time of need.
Hebrews 4:15-16

Sound familiar? Do you remember Day 4 of last week? God transfers His strength to those who are close to Him, not to those far away.

3. PRAY, SISTER, PRAY.

Watch and pray that you may not enter into temptation. The spirit indeed is willing, but the flesh is weak.
Matthew 26:41

Pray then like this . . . "Lead us not into temptation, but deliver us from evil."
Matthew 6:9,13

4. FIGHT TEMPTATION LIKE NOBODY'S BUSINESS.

Resist the devil, and he will flee from you.
James 4:7

I want to stop here for a second. The context of this passage implies that when we humble ourselves before God, He will give us strength to resist the devil. To humble ourselves is to choose obedience. Choosing obedience may mean several things for you right now.

It may mean you place yourself in an accountability relationship because you are not yet able to choose obedience on your own. Or maybe you need some practical advice about what it means to avoid temptation.

You can practice the following:
- avoiding places where your temptation hangs out
- ignoring the phone if your temptation is calling
- forgoing activities that stir up your temptation
- being mindful that loneliness may encourage your temptation
- surrounding yourself with people who are committed to your obedience
- keeping yourself in the presence of God and His people, His places, His words, and His glory

It may also help you to hear that learning to walk in obedience is some days a victory and other days another learning experience. Just keep learning and don't give up practicing a new step of obedience.

And then, oh so graciously, our Lord does not leave us without blessing:

> *Blessed is the man who remains steadfast under trial, for when he has stood the test he will receive the crown of life, which God has promised to those who love him.*
> *James 1:12*

A LITTLE STRONGER—As long as I live on this earth, I will encounter temptations that are common to everyone. But not one of those temptations can overtake me. God has made an escape. I want to learn His way out.

WITH STRESS/ANXIETY

About a year ago, I began to experience some kind of tightening just underneath my ribcage. I assumed I'd pulled a muscle. But eventually the random, tight sensation had my attention. It was obviously not just a pulled muscle. It didn't bother me all the time and some days not at all. Much as I tried, I couldn't decide what was causing this thing or where it actually occurred. One day it'd be a little higher, and the next day, a little lower. I pushed and prodded, but felt nothing. No lump. No tenderness.

So I finally did what any modern woman would do. I Googled. An ache under your rib is bad. You might actually be a goner if you have a tightening near your rib, especially the right rib.

So off to the doctor I went. She said, "Hmm, I'm not sure what this could be."

So the testing began. Ultrasound. Blood work. Colonoscopy. For about two months, I went here, there, and yonder. Filled out the same forms. Described the same tight feeling to doctors, nurses, lab techs, and anybody else who asked, "Why are you here today?" Then, when I woke up from the colonoscopy, the doctor said, "All clear. Everything has checked out great. My best guess about the tightening is stress. See you in ten years."

Stress? I thought I was doing a great job juggling my crazy life. Someone explained it like this: "Yep, we can all pretend we're doing fine with life's stress. But the body will usually betray you and tell the truth."

My mom was very sick at the time. It was the end of school with exams, parties, and recitals. We launched our first women's conference. My son was graduating. Our family was traveling to Bolivia. Each child had camps, mission trips, and two-a-day sports practices. We had college orientation, then we added an international student to our family. On top of all that, we had weeds in the flowerbed, teenage sleepovers, and attempts at something new for dinner.

I thought I was having the time of my life, but now I think about it, I guess there was a little stress.

How about you? Do you have any little stressors in your life?

GOD'S STRENGTH OVER MY STRESS

I love the Lord with all my heart and long to love Him more. Every day, I pray to be growing and changing and learning how to make this journey for His glory. But I live on this fallen planet in a fallen body. I get headaches, an occasional stuffy nose, and a weird tight feeling at my rib. The truth is glaring. I'm just a human being whose life keeps proving how much I need a Savior.

If I happen to forget and begin acting like I'm managing this fallen world OK, my body and soul are faithful to remind me that I am not strong enough. In fact, God never intended for me, or you, to be strong enough on our own. We were made to need Him, run to Him, and surrender to Him.

As I see it, we have two choices when confronted with the stress of our lives. We can succumb to greater anxiety, fear, and pain and continue to rack our minds for solutions and exhaust our bodies with worry. Then try to squeeze answers from other fallen people whose stress is probably greater than ours. Or we can choose to surrender our stress to the strength of God. HE. IS. STRONGER.

While many Scriptures cover God's stronger peace, I've chosen the beautiful words Paul wrote to the Philippians. Let's take this passage phrase by phrase, considering how these verses instruct us to choose God's strength when stress fills the soul:

> *The Lord is at hand.*
> *Philippians 4:5*

Paul reminds us the Lord is near. He may be speaking of God's continual presence or His soon return, but either way, this truth gives comfort and renews our awareness.

When I finally realize I'm stressed, it's usually because I have momentarily forgotten whose I am, to whom I belong, and who holds all that concerns me. Several times in my marriage,

THE BIBLE SPEAKS TO OUR STRESS

Be gracious to me, O LORD, for I am in distress; my eye is wasted from grief; my soul and my body also. For my life is spent with sorrow, and my years with sighing; my strength fails because of my iniquity, and my bones waste away. (Psalm 31:9-10)

Anxiety in a man's heart weighs him down, but a good word makes him glad. (Proverbs 12:25)

When the cares of my heart are many, your consolations cheer my soul. (Psalm 94:19)

Therefore do not be anxious, saying, "What shall we eat?" or "What shall we drink?" or "What shall we wear?" ... [Y]our heavenly Father knows that you need them all. But seek first the kingdom of God and his righteousness, and all these things will be added to you. (Matthew 6:31-33)

Humble yourselves, therefore, under the mighty hand of God so that at the proper time he may exalt you, casting all your anxieties on him, because he cares for you. (1 Peter 5:6-7)

I have worriedly said to my husband, "Oh, Lord, help us." From this calm place of remembrance inside of him, Scott has always responded, "And He is."

Every time Scott has said that to me, I have smiled at him with great relief and said something like, "Whew. Hallelujah. Amen." His reminder always prompts me to re-engage my soul with the Lord, to remember His promises and His strength to me.

> *Do not be anxious about anything.*
> *Philippians 4:6*

You should know these words were not written as a suggestion or a nice idea to try when you're having a good day. "Do not be anxious" is a command. I know what you're thinking, *How in the world can a weak, stressed woman choose not to be anxious about anything?* Thank goodness the apostle is ahead of us with an answer:

> *But in everything by prayer and supplication with thanksgiving let your*
> *requests be made known to God.*
> *Philippians 4:6*

Prayer is the Bible's cure for anxiety and stress. And here's the glory of it all. Christian prayer is not just a focused yoga pose. It is not a quiet moment of reflection. Nor is it meditating on good thoughts to a higher power of your choice. For the Christian, prayer and supplication mean earnest pleas sent from your heart right to the compassionate heart of our Almighty God. Prayer is the means by which a stressed-out woman connects with the power of God.

Paul says we are supposed to pray with thanksgiving, which means we know in advance that God is stronger than anything causing our stress. I am little and too many tiny things can become stress to me. But our God is big, and I pray with thankfulness that nothing in my world is stronger than God.

We've been talking about our stress, so take a few minutes to list your stressors. If you're like me, you'll want to use your journal to list them. If you're like my son, you'll just want to draw doodles that represent your stressors. Either way, let 'em rip!

Now here's the supplication part. Look back at the list you just made and spend the next minutes appealing to God in prayer, asking Him to change each situation. No need to tell Him how to do it. Just humble yourself with your earnest requests.

> *And the peace of God, which surpasses all understanding, will guard your hearts and your minds in Christ Jesus.*
> *Philippians 4:7*

The only lasting stress relief I have ever known is the peace of God. Paul tells us three things about the peace God gives when the anxious pray.

1. THIS IS A DIVINE PEACE. The "peace of God," is an *omni*-God kind of peace. All the peace needed. For all circumstances. Available to all who believe in Him. When you have the divine peace of God, there is freedom from your stress.

All kinds of things in this world promise to give you peace. What is the difference between worldly peace and divine peace?

2. THIS PEACE TRANSCENDS ALL UNDERSTANDING. We will not understand how the divine peace of God relieves our stress, but it does.

3. THIS PEACE WILL GUARD YOUR HEART AND YOUR MIND. Paul chose a military term to communicate a peace that stands guard, keeping out anything trying to bring stress or anxiety.

> *You keep him in perfect peace whose mind is stayed on you, because he trusts in you.*
> *Isaiah 26:3*

To keep the divine peace of God, Paul instructs us to trade our anxious thought for new ones.

Finally, brothers, whatever is true, whatever is honorable, whatever is just, whatever is pure, whatever is lovely, whatever is commendable, if there is any excellence, if there is anything worthy of praise, think about these things. What you have learned and received and heard and seen in me—practice these things, and the God of peace will be with you.
Philippians 4:8-9

This often overlooked part of the passage is a biggie. Do you want to keep living in peace? Will you let God make you stronger than the stress you encounter? Then some changes in your thinking need to happen: anxious, worried, fretful thoughts need to go out; and honorable, just, pure, lovely, commendable, excellent, praiseworthy thoughts come in.

One more time, read the last sentence of Philippians 4:9. What are we supposed to keep doing?

We're supposed to practice exchanging our anxious thoughts to keep living in God's peace. It's a biggie, I know.

When a woman changes the way she thinks about her life, she is taking a huge, difficult step of spiritual maturity. It's hard to do. I have dear friends who have been saying the same anxious, worried things to me for at least twenty years because it's been too difficult for them to change their old worry patterns. Or maybe they never really tried.

Jesus had some strong words about why this kind of person won't live in peace. Their heart is full of thorns.

As for what was sown among thorns, this is the one who hears the word, but the cares of the world and the deceitfulness of riches choke the word, and it proves unfruitful.
Matthew 13:22

How is God asking you to change the way you think?

If you continue to let the stress and worries of this world choke His instruction, then you will live everyday without peace. You have effectively decided that your stress trumps God's power to answer.

The woman who daily refuses to make the exchange will live a miserable, unfruitful life. Ugh. Hope that didn't make you more stressed. Maybe we can begin "thinking about these things" by adding truth to truth. God's truth added to our truth might go something like this:

These worries I carry are legitimate concerns, but God is faithful and good.

This situation I'm facing is awful and scary, but God is with me and promises He'll never leave me.

How can you add God's truth to your truth today?

This _____ is _____.

But God is _____.

Fretting is sinful if you are a child of God. Get back to God by confessing that you've been thinking your circumstances are too much for Him. Ask for forgiveness and then say, "Lord, I take You into my calculation as the biggest factor NOW!"

A LITTLE STRONGER—I commit to change my thinking. First, I add God's truth about peace to the truth of my stress. Then, with practice, new thoughts about peace begin to replace my old focus on my stress. Finally, I continue practicing, mostly thinking about God's peace, rarely thinking about my stress.

WITH DOUBT

My son Grayson is a freshman at Liberty University. Grayson is a passionate follower of Jesus. He is an artist, a philosophical thinker, and a very happy, optimistic person. But sometime around his junior year of high school, Grayson began struggling with doubt. Doubts about God, Jesus, Scripture, and his own imperfect faith.

Honestly, I had been expecting this season for him. He is hungry for truth, and whenever anyone longs for truth, struggles and flat-out battles with doubt often result.

Grayson is modeling for our family how to face doubts with integrity. He has not turned away from God or his connection with other believers, but he brings his questions into the light, asking and searching until the new challenge in his head has been satisfied with truth and revelation. I smile when I think about Grayson in the middle of these searching years. I guess it's because I did the same thing.

In one of our conversations, Grayson told me his struggles with doubt made him afraid his faith would be diminished somehow. He feared doubt would steal the joy he had with Jesus. Doubt does have that power. But doubt loses its power in the light of God's truth, so we don't have to be afraid when we take our doubts to God.

> *For many Christians, merely having doubts of any kind can be scary. They wonder whether their questions disqualify them being a follower of Christ. They feel insecure because they're not sure whether it's permissible to express uncertainty about God, Jesus, or the Bible. So they keep their questions to themselves—and inside, unanswered, they grow and fester . . . until they eventually succeed in choking out their faith.*[7] —Lee Strobel

Because my own season of searching made my faith stronger, I have never been afraid of Grayson's questions or doubts. The questions that plagued me were settled by the truth of God's Word, so I want my son to take his doubts and search for the truth. Study the Word. Read great spiritual thinkers and scholars. And wrestle each doubt to the ground until he has God's answer.

One thing I am absolutely sure of, God's Word can stand up to Grayson's doubts. And mine. And yours. Most great followers of God have wrestled with their doubts until God's truth won. I hope you'd like to do a little wrestling today.

I am encouraged that many great people of faith have faced doubt.

Choose one of the great doubters below and read his story. If you want to cast your net a little wider, read as many as you'd like. No matter which you choose, the questions below are for all.

John the Baptist	Matthew 3; 11:2-3
Peter	Matthew 14:22-33
Thomas	John 20:24-29
Father of the epileptic boy	Mark 9:14-27
Gideon	Judges 6:11-40

Based on what you read, describe your doubter's relationship with the Lord before his doubt was revealed.

What was the nature of his doubt?

How did the Lord respond to his doubt?

Do you get the idea that the Lord is patient with our questions and our ability to reason with things we cannot yet fully understand? On this earth, we see only in part. We know only in part. The Lord shows us in these verses that He is graciously patient when we struggle with doubt. The Lord was not angry with their doubts; He only wanted them to believe.

- John the Baptist doubted Jesus was the Messiah.
- Peter doubted the power of Jesus.
- Thomas doubted the resurrection of Jesus.
- The father of the epileptic doubted Jesus was able to heal.
- Gideon doubted God's promise to use him.

I imagine each one of these great doubters thought, *What if I'm wrong? What if I've been tricked? What if He's not really God?* These great Bible doubters aren't the only ones to struggle with skepticism and waning faith. But I'm sure you already know that.

THE CAUSE OF OUR DOUBTS

If we live long enough, most of us will experience seasons of difficult circumstances, darkness, sorrow, or spiritual oppression. Charles Spurgeon says:

> *God has not made for his people a smooth path to heaven. Before they are crowned they must fight; before they can enter the celestial city fulfill a weary pilgrimage.*[8]

The weary follower of God can struggle with doubt for many reasons:

- Loneliness might cause us ask, *Have I been abandoned? Was God ever really with me?*
- Overwhelming personal trials can cause us to doubt God's goodness.
- Satan's lies make us wonder if we're accepted by God or loved at all.
- The weight of our sin can feel so great that we question how God can keep us.
- Our weary heart can become hard when we can't "feel God."
- Lack of desire to fellowship with God can lead to doubt.

Beyond personal doubts, we also struggle with intellectual doubt. We glance at the day's headlines and wonder, *Is God good when so much suffering fills the world?*

We need to know that many great scholars came to faith in Christ when they sought truth for their intellectual doubts. Lee Strobel is just one example of an intellectual doubter whose search for truth led him to God. A lawyer and journalist, Strobel was an atheist who decided to investigate the story of Jesus. He determined to do all the research necessary to disprove the claims of the Bible. You can read the results of his research in his book, *The Case for Christ*.

I'm going to spoil the story, but in his quest to prove the man from Nazareth was not the Christ, Lee Strobel became a passionate follower of Jesus. With regard to intellectual doubts, Strobel quotes Ravi Zacharias:

> *A man rejects God neither because of intellectual demands nor because of the scarcity of evidence. A man rejects God because of a moral resistance that refuses to admit his need for God.*

Do you struggle with any of the reasons for doubt listed above? If not, what causes your doubt?

> *It were enough to make the mightiest heart doubt, if it should look only at things that are seen. He that is nearest to the kingdom of heaven would have cause to droop and die if he had nothing to look at but that which eye can see and ear can hear.[9]* —Charles Spurgeon

STRONGER THAN OUR DOUBTS

The likelihood is great that I will not have answers for all your doubts, but I am not worried; I know the God who does. Even though I know Him only in part, I am learning to trust Him fully with what I do not understand. I trust He holds the answers to your struggles. I also trust He will be faithful to deliver you from the struggle of doubt if you will search for Him.

Hear these promises from God:

> *You will seek me and find me, when you seek me with all your heart. I will be found by you, declares the LORD.*
> *Jeremiah 29:13-14*

> *I love those who love me, and those who seek me diligently find me.*
> *Proverbs 8:17*

> *Ask, and it will be given to you; seek, and you will find; knock, and it will be opened to you. For everyone who asks receives, and the one who seeks finds, and to the one who knocks it will be opened.*
> *Matthew 7:7-8*

Maybe today, some of your doubts might be settled by this observation from Matthew 14:22-31: From a boat, the disciples looked and saw Jesus walking on water. Peter doubted and asked, "Lord, if it is you, command me to come to you on the water."

Jesus said, "Come," and Peter got out of the boat and walked on the water to Jesus.

The Scripture says when Peter saw the wind, he became afraid and began to sink. Jesus took his hand and lifted him up saying, "O you of little faith, why did you doubt?"

Spurgeon writes about Peter:

> *He might have traversed the leagues of the Atlantic, he might have crossed the broad Pacific, if he could but have kept his eye on Christ, and ne'er a billow would have yielded to his tread, but he might have been drowned in a very brook if he began to look at [his circumstances] . . . forgetting the Great Head and Master of the Universe who had bidden him walk the sea.*[10]

Today, where are you looking? At your trouble, your circumstances, or your understanding?

Are you looking only at what you can see? Are you willing you turn your eyes back to the One who called you—the One who lives inside of you and promises to sustain you? Jesus' Word is stronger than anything you can see or feel, but you can forget about His strength when looking at yourself and where you're walking. Maybe today, all that is needed is the turn of your gaze.

I truly believe if your heart does not find peace in these pages, it is not because of God, His character, or His truth. The problem is either the messenger (me) or the receiver (you). Thankfully, God is not frustrated with either one of us. He wants only for us to believe.

And so, my sister, I pray you'll bring your doubts to God. He is able to settle each one. You will find Him when you will search for Him with all of your heart. He never turns an honest doubter away.

A LITTLE STRONGER—I resolve to seek God and find His truth. I stand on Jesus' promise today: "You will know the truth and the truth will set you free" (John 8:32).

FINDING DIRECTION FOR MY LIFE

Do you remember *Alice's Adventures in Wonderland*? At one point, Alice comes to a fork in the road and asks the Cheshire Cat which direction she should take.

> *"That depends a good deal on where you want to get to," said the Cat.*
> *"I don't much care where—," said Alice.*
> *"Then it doesn't matter which way you walk," said the Cat.*

If you don't care, finding your way in life isn't a struggle. But when you begin to care about living for God's glory, the struggle to find your way begins.

College was a no-brainer for me. I'm embarrassed to say I don't even remember praying about it. I had been accepted at the University of North Carolina, so that's where I was going. No one on either side of my family had graduated from college, so I would be the first. My post-college plans were pretty simple: go home to Greensboro and spend the rest of my life learning my dad's trucking business.

I hadn't thought much about my plan because there was nothing to think about. The plan was assumed by me and by my family. The only reason for my going to college was to come home a little smarter to help with the family business. My senior year, I felt sorry for all the kids who plowed through job interviews and the ones who didn't really know what they wanted to do in life. Not me; I just had to go home and get to work.

At home I began volunteering with the youth group at my church. God used those goofy, precious kids to blow up my plan. I fell in love with the kids, with God's Word, and with ministry. I had no idea something could light up your soul the way teaching the Bible did for me. My heart responded to the call to live for God's glory, and my struggle to find direction began in earnest.

For months, I wrestled and cried and prayed and worried. I talked to people and made appointments with pastors. I journaled and fasted and worshiped. Eventually my earthly dad blessed me with his words, "For months I have watched God calling you into ministry. I'm honored He'd use my daughter. I want you to go."

For a long time after that I occasionally struggled with whispers of regret. Shoot, if I had known what I was going to do with my life, I would have taken a writing class. Or majored in speech. Or gone to Bible college. Or prayed about it sooner!

Now I can see God's patience with my searching—His enduring and pursuing love. He is so gracious to come and say, "No, not that way. Over here." God is stronger than all our struggles with direction, our wrong turns and circuitous routes. He is able to guide each one of us—even those of us who feel completely lost. And I'm so very grateful for that.

Have you ever gone down a road only to have God surprise you with a sharp change in direction? If so, describe it.

WHEN YOU DON'T KNOW WHAT TO DO

When I don't know what to do, the best thing for me is to pull out my Bible and follow the path of someone who did. Let's take a quick look at a few verses in Nehemiah, the story of a prophet who asked God what to do.

Read Nehemiah 1:1-11 below.

> *The words of Nehemiah the son of Hacaliah. Now it happened in the month of Chislev, in the twentieth year, as I was in Susa the citadel, that Hanani, one of my brothers, came with certain men from Judah. And I asked them concerning the Jews who escaped, who had survived the exile, and concerning Jerusalem. And they said to me, "The remnant there in the province who had survived the exile is in great trouble and shame. The wall of Jerusalem is broken down, and its gates are destroyed by fire." As soon as I heard these words I sat down and wept and mourned for days, and I continued fasting and praying before the God of heaven. And I said, "O LORD God of heaven, the great and awesome God who keeps covenant and steadfast love with those who love him and keep his commandments, let your ear be attentive and your eyes open, to hear the prayer of your servant that I now pray before you day and night for the people of Israel your servants, confessing the sins of the people of Israel, which we have sinned against you. Even I and my father's house have sinned. We have acted very corruptly against you and have not kept the commandments, the statutes, and the rules that you commanded your servant Moses. Remember*

the word that you commanded your servant Moses, saying, 'If you are unfaithful, I will scatter you among the peoples, but if you return to me and keep my commandments and do them, though your outcasts are in the uttermost parts of heaven, from there I will gather them and bring them to the place that I have chosen, to make my name dwell there.' They are your servants and your people, whom you have redeemed by your great power and by your strong hand. O Lord, let your ear be attentive to the prayer of your servant, and to the prayer of your servants who delight to fear your name, and give success to your servant today, and grant him mercy in the sight of this man."
Now I was cupbearer to the king.

OK, I will *not* point you to four easy steps to knowing God's direction for your life, but based on this passage, I can give you four steps to getting started. When we don't know what to do, we can imitate the followers of God who served Him well, so let's look at what Nehemiah did:

1. NEHEMIAH STUDIED THE SITUATION AND CIRCUMSTANCES (V. 2-3)

You and I can begin the same way. Are you struggling with finding direction for your life? Set aside your emotions, worries, and fears long enough to take a careful inventory of your circumstances.

Where are you struggling with direction right now?

How did you get to this place?

What are the influencing factors that keep you from finding direction?

2. NEHEMIAH HAD COMPASSION FOR THE PEOPLE (V. 4)

Here's an interesting and beautiful element to apply to our personal struggles. It's so very easy to keep our focus on ourselves. Our needs. Our inconvenience. Our desires.

Who are the people you care for who need your compassion?

How might having compassion for those around you give greater insight in the direction God has for your life?

3. NEHEMIAH HUMBLED HIMSELF BEFORE GOD (V. 4)

To humble yourself before God means to lower your importance and make Him higher. To humble yourself is also to surrender your attitude and your personal desires.

> *Humility is nothing but the disappearance of self in the vision that God is all.*[11]
> —Andrew Murray

We all need to humble ourselves over and over. What situation do you face now that challenges you to humble yourself?

4. NEHEMIAH PRAYED (V. 5-11)

In Nehemiah's prayer, he confessed the sin of his nation and then asked God for help. Nehemiah knew that all wisdom comes from God, but it often comes through the counsel of godly people. Wisdom also requires the pursuit of information and knowledge. Ultimately, we long for God's wisdom above all else.

Has a sin played a part in your struggle with direction? Have you been unwilling to consider God's plan? Stubborn? Unrealistic?

Are you willing to turn from that sin to seek His wisdom? In prayer, ask God for all the help you need in finding direction. Jot down the results of your prayer.

THE BLESSING OF SEARCHING FOR YOUR DIRECTION WITH GOD

Our God is not an algorithm to be figured out. He is bigger than formulas. He will not be manipulated or controlled. But those who seek Him will find Him. He is glorified when we submit our lives and dreams to be guided by the principles of His Word.

If we were sitting across from one another today—cups of coffee and Bibles between us—here is what I would tell you about finding your direction in life:

> *Love God and do what you please. —Augustine of Hippo*

How would you explain to a new believer the meaning of Augustine's statement?

WHAT I'VE LEARNED ABOUT FINDING AND FOLLOWING GOD'S DIRECTION:

1. STAY WITH GOD. Stay hidden in Him, clothed with His Word. Live in quick obedience, humble before Him. No matter what struggle you face, God is stronger. The safest place for you and me is with God.

2. IMPULSIVE DECISIONS SOMETIMES PAY OFF, BUT NOT USUALLY. In Scripture, we see God directing us to walk in wisdom and spend time in prayer as we make important decisions. Part of that wisdom means not staying stuck in excessive and paralyzing self-examination.

3. GOOD DECISIONS NEVER CONTRADICT ANYTHING WRITTEN IN GOD'S WORD. Sift your decision through His truth.

4. GOD DOES NOT MAKE HIS WILL A SECRET WITH TRICKS TO KEEP YOU FROM FINDING HIS DIRECTION. Living in His truth and according to His ways is the most direct way to walk in God's will.

5. WHEN YOU BELIEVE GOD IS LEADING YOU, THEN ACT. Take off and go.

6. GO WITH THIS SWEET TRUTH ABOUT GOD'S LOVE: If you stay with God and still make a wrong turn, He will turn you around.

> *He has told you, O man, what is good;*
> *and what does the LORD require of you*
> *but to do justice, and to love kindness,*
> *and to walk humbly with your God?*
> *Micah 6:8*

God is stronger than this challenge. And through this challenge, He is making me stronger.

A LITTLE STRONGER—I will face my struggles about direction and decision-making, letting Jesus be my guide.

VIEWER GUIDE SESSION 3

PSALM 84

STRONGER IN HIM

DAVID FOUND STRENGTH IN GOD.

Psalm 18:32; 28:8; 105:4; 118:14; 119; 138:3

WE ARE STRENGTHENED BY GOD.

Isaiah 12:2; 40:31; 58:11; Jeremiah 16:19; Ephesians 3:16; Philippians 4:13; Colossians 1:11; 2 Thessalonians 3:3

WE ARE STRENGTHENED BY THE GOSPEL.

Colossians 2:6-7,9-10

The_____ that we long for is hidden in the _____ of the _____.

If the Lord has said there is no more _____, then _____ ____ your head.

If the Lord has called you _____, live in it.

When we live in Him, we are _____ to obey from this _____ _____.

The gospel is the _____. Our _____ is the _____ of His power in us.

There is nothing in the _____ that teaches us that what we _____ pre-cedes how we are _____.

We are to be _____ because we are walking in the _____ ____ _____ _____.

GOD IS STRONGER THAN MY BAD NEWS

ASSIGNED TO PLANET EARTH

Just a few days ago, my daughter Taylor texted this prayer request: "Can you pray for my friend Lucy? Her world is falling apart. She just started coming to church for the first time in her life, and I don't want her to get discouraged."

Scott and I began praying for Lucy. Then came the next text: "Mom, do you have any good Bible verses for Lucy?"

Bible verses? Of course I have Bible verses! But what I wanted so much more was to drive to Tennessee and give Lucy a long mom-hug, then sit right beside her and talk to her about the love of God for all of us. I wanted to give her the good news that saves us from the bad news. We have been assigned to live our lives in a fallen world, but we are not without hope.

Now yes, yes, creation sometimes screams a confusing message—fear, pain, grief. Fires burn, rivers flood, winds go hurricane, the earth shudders so hard it levels cities. But you must remember—this was not so in Eden. Mankind fell, surrendering this earth to the evil one. St. Paul says that creation groans for the day of its restoration (see Rom. 8:18-22), making it clear that everything is not as it was meant to be. People come to terrible conclusions when they assume this world is exactly as God intended. (An assumption that has wrought havoc in the sciences.) The earth is broken. Which only makes the beauty that does flow so generously that much more astounding. And reassuring.[1]

—*John Eldredge*

How are you personally affected by the following consequences of the fall?

1. Adam and Eve's sin was assigned (imputed) to all their descendants. Our human nature was corrupted.

2. Adam and Eve immediately lost boldness and joy in the presence of God.

3. After their sin, they experienced fear and shame for the first time.

4. They were sent away from the garden and separated from God.

5. Childbirth would be forever marked by pain and danger.

6. Life on earth would now require difficult and exhausting labor to gather and sustain food, clothing, and shelter.

7. The consequence of their sin was death.

Our very first breath was taken in a world broken by sin. And we arrived in that world with a sin nature we inherited. We did not choose the broken planet or the sin nature we bear, but thankfully, our Lord has chosen to save us from the eternal consequences of both.

Are you feeling the effects of living in this broken place today? If so, how would you describe the effects in these three areas?

1. Physically

2. Relationally

3. Spiritually

THE FALL THAT BROKE THE WORLD

Genesis 1 and 2 tell us God created Adam and Eve and placed them in the garden of Eden. Their bodies, their relationship, and their home were the perfect creation of God. They fellowshipped with God. He met all their physical and emotional needs. Adam and Eve were to live faithful to God, enjoying all the blessings bestowed on them by their Father. In the garden, God gave them one limitation: no eating the fruit from the tree of the knowledge of good and evil.

As you well know, Satan used God's command to tempt Adam and Eve to rebel against God. They willingly disobeyed and sinned. Because God is holy, He imposed consequences for their sin. Adam and Eve fell and all of creation fell with them. The world, and our relationship with God, was broken by their sin.

> *Fall of Man: Transition from a state of moral innocence and favor with God to a state of condemnation and death, which occurred in the history of mankind with Adam's eating of the forbidden fruit.*[2]

The consequences of the fall were not only for Adam and Eve, but extended to all their descendants. That is why you and I encounter the effects of their disobedience.

This afternoon I asked my 17-year-old son, William, to name the top five effects of the fall of man he encounters everyday.

"Mom," he said without looking up, "there are just too many."

William is right: what began as one act of rebellion in the garden has become multiplied sin. A single act of temptation by Satan has become unrestrained evil in the hearts of men.

> *Therefore, just as sin came into the world through one man, and death through sin, and so death spread to all men because all sinned.*
> *Romans 5:12*

In addition to these effects, Satan is still free to roam. In the garden, he tempted two with disastrous consequences. Today, his work continues, multiplied by the sheer numbers of humanity.

GOD IS STRONGER THAN THE FALL OF MAN

Even in Genesis 3, where the account of man's fall is written, we begin to see the saving grace of God. He could have punished Adam and Eve with an immediate death, but He did not. His love for them, even in the garden of great disappointment, endured. His love was stronger than their fall!

As Adam and Eve stand before God in their shame, before He passes judgment, God makes the promise of a Savior. The New Testament describes it this way:

> For as by the one man's disobedience the many were made sinners, so by the one man's obedience the many will be made righteous.
> Romans 5:19

The language in Genesis 3:15 is figurative, so it may be a little hard to understand. Let's take the verse phrase by phrase to gain a strong grasp on what God is promising.

Genesis 3:15 picks up in the middle of God's curse on the serpent (Satan).

> I will put enmity between you and the woman, and between your offspring and her offspring.

Keep in mind this curse is for Satan. When you read the word *enmity*, think of it as "declaring war." In this figurative style of writing, the word *woman* represents "all her offspring or descendants." (Note: this curse does not mean women *will* be afraid of snakes . . . though I wholeheartedly endorse that aversion.)

The Message paraphrased the passage as follows:

> I'm [God is] declaring war between you [Satan] and the Woman [her descendants], between your offspring and hers.

The first promise of this passage is there will be a perpetual struggle between satanic forces and mankind. The sin and devastation we see all around us is evidence that this spiritual warfare continues to this day.

Who are the offspring of Satan?

Who are the offspring of the woman?

Next, God promises victory in the battle over Satan. With these words, God foretells the coming of His Son, a descendant of the woman who comes in victory over Satan and his offspring.

> *He shall bruise your head, and you shall bruise his heel.*
> *Genesis 3:15*

The bruising is the battle between Satan and the promised Redeemer. But even though Satan strikes at the heel to cripple us, Jesus gives the final strike to the head to free us from the judgment of sin and Satan's torment on earth. The New Testament expresses the same truth:

> *The God of peace will soon crush Satan under your feet.*
> *Romans 16:20*

> *For as in Adam all die, so also in Christ shall all be made alive.*
> *1 Corinthians 15:22*

NOT WITHOUT HOPE

My sweet sister, I imagine you are like me on occasion: so weary of our sin natures, the reality of Satan, and this broken world with its pain, disease, and disasters. We have been assigned to live on this earth, but our Father has not left us without hope. God has given us the artillery of His Word, the army of His Church, the strength of His Holy Spirit, and the victory of His Son, Jesus.

A LITTLE STRONGER—The struggle to face bad news in a fallen world will not overcome me. The mercy of God has provided a Redeemer and I have hope.

WHEN BAD NEWS COMES

Everyone eventually wakes up to a day when bad news comes. A diagnosis. A call in the night. A notice posted at work. A police officer at your door. In what feels like a very short life, I've already had several times like that. I bet you have too.

Just two months ago, bad news came about my mom. It was 8:30 Friday morning. I was in the Philadelphia airport, walking to board a flight to Maryland. Daddy called from the hospital and said, "Mama's doctor wants to talk to you."

The night before, I left my parents at the hospital around 10:00. Daddy and I were both grateful because, though very sick with ovarian cancer, Mama seemed better that Thursday. The three of us sat together in her room until bedtime, talking and laughing. Before I left, Mama told me where to find her recipe for a really good jambalaya. I told her I'd come straight to her from the airport on Sunday, and we'd get ready for a Thanksgiving feast.

As I drove home from the hospital that night, I was struck by Mama's connectedness in our conversation. She just kept looking at me like she loved me soooo much. She was completely interested in everything I had to say. Today as I'm remembering that precious night, one hand is trying to type while the other hand uses the corner of the bed sheet to wipe my tears. I am undone thinking about the sweetness in her blue eyes.

The next morning found me leaning against an airport wall, attempting to hear a doctor say, "Angela, God is calling your mom home. She has hours or days left here."

Even though Mama was sick, we were all shocked. No one had ever told us the end was so close. On Saturday, Mama waited for all of her family to get to the hospital. Then she waited a few more hours until her 51st wedding anniversary on Sunday. Then her work was done. Her family was with her when she went to heaven.

BEFORE THE BAD NEWS

I cannot say which day was the worst: the day I heard mama had ovarian cancer, the day my sister drowned, the day my aunt was killed in an airplane crash, or the day mama went to heaven. And until I am with the Lord, there will be more bad news. Jesus says it this way:

I have said these things to you, that in me you may have peace. In the world you will have tribulation.
John 16:33

Notice Jesus says, "you will have," not "if you have" or "maybe you'll have." Tribulation is defined as trouble, suffering, or distress. And Jesus says experiencing tribulation in this world is unavoidable.

But just as trouble is promised, so is another assurance to believers:

But take heart; I have overcome the world.
John 16:33

Do you need to reach out your hands and take hold of this promise today? The certain troubles of this world will not overcome believers. Those who trust Jesus to overcome this world can live through tribulation in His peace.

Can you describe for me one case in which God has shown you peace in the midst of tribulation?

The truth of this passage holds no matter when you come to understand its strength. But how I long for you to possess this truth before bad news comes. The sadness of tribulation is tough all by itself. But to encounter tribulation without the hope of Christ—I can only imagine the depths of that despair.

Jesus originally spoke these words in Greek, using the imperative mood, which signifies a command. My children know the intent of my instruction based on my tone. Jesus' tone in this case was a command. He wants us to know what is possible for those who obey His command.

Have you taken hold of the courage for believers through Jesus? Or have you heard but not yet taken hold?

I have no idea how someone can face this world with its bad news and horrible evil without the hope of Jesus Christ. The Bible says it this way:

Who is it that overcomes the world except the one who believes that Jesus is the Son of God?
1 John 5:5

When you become a follower of Christ, Colossians promises that

Your life is hidden with Christ in God . . . you have been filled in Him.
Colossians 3:3; 2:10

From the moment we believe in Christ as Savior, we are hidden in Him and filled by Him. Next week, we'll talk more about what it means to live in Him, but for today, I want you to know the strength to face bad news is provided in Christ. What we need—spiritually, emotionally, and even physically—was bought for us on the cross.

And it gets better! Not only are we hidden in Christ and filled by Christ,

Christ in you [is] the hope of glory.
Colossians 1:27

Right here, Sister, is where we must pitch our tent and camp our souls. Christ in me is my hope.

When headlines promise doom and destruction,

Christ in me is my hope.

When the doctor calls with a desperate diagnosis,

Christ in me is my hope.

When a good child chooses his way,

Christ in me is my hope.

When death comes too soon,

> Christ in me is my hope.

When I am abandoned, without one close friend, left all alone,

> Christ in me is my hope.

When the people who should have loved did not,

> Christ in me is my hope.

Before bad news comes, consider where you are. If you have been hidden in Christ, then Christ in you can teach you to do the following:

- Take courage into your soul because He has overcome every trial we will face.
- Become a woman who withstands the trouble of this world, filled with the peace that comes from believing in Him.
- Let the strength of God's promise become your strength. Possess it. Stand on it when bad news comes. Build your life around it. Live in this fallen world . . . stronger.

Before you lift your head to see what's next in your day,

- stop your mind for a minute,
- picture yourself hidden in the strong arms of Christ, and
- praise Him for the safety and peace He gives there.

A LITTLE STRONGER—I am hidden in Christ. I can face bad news in grace and peace because I trust the One who has saved me.

DAY 3

DISEASE

This week of our study is a tough one. But the topics we're tackling are real life. God gave the Bible to guide our journey, even when we face bad news. So I encourage you not to shrink back from this week. It will be powerful and peace-giving to have the truth of Scripture tucked inside your heart when struggles come.

Though he slay me, yet will I trust him.
Job 13:15 (KJV)

Today's topic may take an unexpected turn for you. We are not going to talk about disease— not its causes, remedies, or strategies for coping. Encountering disease is certain. Either I, or someone I love, will face a battle with a dreaded disease. It's unfair and sad and downright awful. I grieve every Facebook post I read that announces another diagnosis and treatment plan for someone I love. Each post reminds me how much I long for the home where we were made to dwell.

What I'm going to ask of you today is what I'm asking of and praying for myself. I want to learn to trust the God of my salvation so completely that in disease, in loss, and in confusion as to what in the world God is doing, my soul will learn to say, "Yet I will trust Him."

FROM BAD TO WORSE
The prophet Habakkuk wrote three little chapters in the Old Testament, but it's their power-packed ending that has my attention today. First, let me tell you the backstory.

At the heart of the Book of Habakkuk is a perplexed prophet having an honest dialog with God. He asks questions familiar to all of us—questions of how long and why.

The world looked grim to Habakkuk. All he could see was international crisis and national corruption, with everything going from bad to worse. The prophet pleaded with God to make things right. He wanted divine justice. Divine judgment. Divine yelling. Anything. He just wanted God to make wrong things right. This morning's headlines and social media posts stir the same questions in our hearts.

Are people you know asking God how long and why? About what?

Most of this prophet's book goes back and forth. Habakkuk questions. God answers. Then Habakkuk questions God's answers, and God answers yet again. But in chapter 2, in one of God's answers, we read the words at the heart of Habakkuk's message:

> *The righteous shall live by his faith.*
> *Habakkuk 2:4*

Here's what we see happening with Habakkuk. When he looked at the world, he was filled with fear, doubt, and worry. (Sound familiar?) But when he turned to God, he was assured God is present and in control. God is at work accomplishing His purposes on earth. Habakkuk learned God is sovereign and, even in the midst of suffering, He can be trusted. He told Habakkuk those who follow God will have to live by their faith.

Is it hard for you to hear God say, "Trust Me" when . . .

> *you don't understand?*

> *life is unfair?*

> *the good guys lose and the bad guys celebrate?*

> *disease comes to your family or to your own body?*

How do you tend to respond to such times?

God responded to Habakkuk's questions with such power, authority, and assurance that Habakkuk wrote this response:

> *Though the fig tree should not blossom, nor fruit be on the vines, the produce of the olive fail and the fields yield no food, the flock be cut off from the fold and there be no herd in the stalls, yet I will rejoice in the LORD; I will take joy in the God of my salvation. GOD, the Lord, is my strength; he makes my feet like the deer's; he makes me tread on my high places.*
> *Habakkuk 3:17-19*

Habakkuk is so convinced God has not abandoned His people that he essentially says, "If everything is taken away from me, if the awful things I imagine come true, I will still rejoice in the Lord anyway."

Oh my. Did your heart just stop? I think mine did. Yet, I will rejoice. That is my prayer.

Reread Habakkuk 3:17-19. Why would Habakkuk rejoice?

If the worst thing happened, where would Habakkuk find the strength to rejoice?

I almost can't speak. Today we are blessed to know so much more than Habakkuk did when he was writing.

- He did not witness the arrival of the promised Savior, Jesus.
- He did not hear the words Jesus spoke or see the resurrected Christ.

But Habakkuk heard God's voice, saw God's vision, and understood the ultimate outcome for all who believe. From that place of trust he determined, *Yet, I will rejoice.* It was all settled for Habakkuk. No matter what came, no matter what his eyes saw, his heart would trust in God.

Notice what's happening here. This is more than deciding to tough it out in bad times; Habakkuk decided to choose joy in the God of his salvation no matter what.

May the same be said of you and me.

Please do not misinterpret my heart in today's teaching. No one rejoices in the diagnosis of disease or the battle against disease. We grieve and weep and groan under the weight of such a burden.

But I have seen women face disease with a whole-hearted trust in the Lord, and I have watched women battle disease without Him. If I am able to choose, I pray that no matter what comes, I will rejoice.

Does that sound crazy? Do you believe the joy of our salvation can give the strength to rejoice even when the worst thing happens?

GOD, THE LORD, IS MY STRENGTH

When Habakkuk spoke of strength in this passage, he chose the strongest names for God available to him. The Hebrew he used was *yahweh ădōnāy* or "Sovereign Lord." He wanted us to understand the power and majesty of the God who is able to give us strength.

Do you know a person battling disease and still trusting God?

What are the characteristics of that kind of faith?

Whom have I in heaven but you? And there is nothing on earth that I desire besides you. My flesh and my heart may fail, but God is the strength of my heart and my portion forever.
Psalm 73:25-26

Our bodies will all fail and many of them fall prey to disease. But God is stronger than our diseases. Will you and I live in His strength if that day comes to us?

A LITTLE STRONGER—I will trust Yahweh Adonai to give me strength to rejoice even if the worst comes.

DEATH AND DYING

As a writer of Bible studies, I never envisioned a day when the title of my lesson would be "Death and Dying." Max Lucado writes about these things better than most of us ever could, so I always thought we should leave these topics to Max. He's a pastor and all, with funerals and such, so he's had a lot more practice at knowing what to say. Or not say.

Today I am stranded on a sofa in South Africa. My Max Lucado library is at home on my shelf and this hotel is without Internet access, or I would certainly be searching for his thoughts. So when I opened this document and saw those words staring at me, I did the only thing I could do. I prayed. *Oh Lord, show me what to tell them.*

I'm not sure God has ever answered me so fast. Before I finished praying, I knew in my spirit that there was only one thing to write. It was like the Lord was saying, *Angela, are you kidding Me? What's with you dreading today's topic? This is the really, really good news of great joy! This is the biggest deal ever! THIS is what they need to know more than anything. Death is not king, I AM. The grave is not the destination, I AM. I AM stronger than death and stronger than the fear of death. Tell them the good news, baby girl, and then tell them again!*

Jesus Christ Himself is the good news and no one said it better:

> *Jesus said to her, "I am the resurrection and the life. Whoever believes in me, though he die, yet shall he live, and everyone who lives and believes in me shall never die. Do you believe this?"*
> *John 11:25-26*

"Whoever believes in me, though he die, yet shall he live." That is the really, really good news of great joy. Death does not have the final say!

How about you? Do you dread today's topic? Maybe, like me, you'd rather not revisit the sadness of losing someone you loved. Or do you feel fear when someone mentions dying?

Recently, I watched the television interview of a woman given three months to live after the diagnosis of incurable brain cancer. She amazed everyone with her upbeat attitude, telling the interviewer, "Keep your chin up and don't go to the funeral—mine or yours or your loved ones—until the day of the funeral because you will miss the life that you have left." Then she added, "Besides, we're all terminal, you know. Death is certain for all of us."

She was right. We are all terminal. Romans 6:23 states simply our predicament:

The wages of sin is death.

In other words, we all receive the same penalty for our sin—death. Mercifully, the verse doesn't stop there:

But the free gift of God is eternal life in Christ Jesus our Lord.

The whole Bible testifies God is stronger than everything. And even though He didn't have to, God graciously sent His Son to prove He is stronger than death.

For God so loved the world that He gave His only Son, that whoever believes in Him should not perish but have eternal life.
John 3:16

Colossians 2:13-14 tells us that trusting Jesus conquers death. I've paraphrased the passage with some of my own wording so you can see the application more clearly, but the passage remains true to its original intent:

When you believe in Jesus, you are forgiven all your trespasses. Jesus does this by canceling the record of debt that stood against you with its legal demands. This He set aside, nailing it to the cross. So that you, who were once dead because of sin, have been made alive together with Him.

When anyone believes in Jesus, what happens?

How does Jesus forgive our trespasses (sins)?

Where did Jesus nail our debt so that it could be forgiven once and for all?

Sin makes us spiritually dead and promises us a physical death. What happens to our death after we have believed in Jesus?

I never tire of hearing someone say, "Jesus did not come to make bad people good. He came to made dead people alive!" Our fate was so much worse than being bad. We were doomed to death because of sin, but in Christ, we have been promised life eternal. When we choose Christ, we choose Christ's victory over death. Read the insightful words of G. C. "Red" Jones:

> *When a free human being uses his freedom to reject the truth of God, and to refuse to relate rightly with him, then there is no alternative except to allow him to do so. In making this choice, man becomes responsible for the results of separation from God. He lives his life in this world without God, and when he dies, God will not pick him up against his will and drag him into a place so drastically different from the kind of person he has chosen to become.*[3]

PROMISES TO BELIEVERS

Because of Jesus, you and I do not have to live in fear of death or dying. We can hold fast to the promises God makes to believers. God is stronger than death and stronger than your fears. Read these reassuring words from pastor and teacher, Charles Spurgeon:

> *There is an essential difference between the decease of the godly and the death of the ungodly. Death comes to the ungodly man as a penal infliction, but to the righteous as a summons to his Father's palace: to the sinner it is an execution, to the saint an undressing. Death to the wicked is the King of terrors: death to the saint is the end of terrors, the commencement of glory.*[4]

The Bible makes promises to believers concerning death. As you study the following passages, rewrite each promise for yourself. You can see how I rewrote the first one.

Fear not, I am the first and the last, and the living one. I died, and behold I
am alive forevermore, and I have the keys of Death and Hades.
Revelation 1:17-18

Realizing that he would soon be gone from this world, one day Moody said to a friend, "Someday you will read in the papers that D. L. Moody of Northfield is dead. Don't you believe a word of it.

"At that moment I shall be more alive than I am now. I shall have gone higher, that is all—out of this old clay tenement into a house that is immortal, a body that sin cannot touch, that sin cannot taint, a body fashioned into His glorious body. I was born in the flesh in 1837; I was born of the Spirit in 1856. That which is born of the flesh may die; that which is born of the Spirit will live forever."[5]

My paraphrase: My death has already been defeated by Jesus.

Death is swallowed up in victory. O death, where is your victory? O death, where is your sting? . . . Thanks be to God, who gives us the victory through our Lord Jesus Christ.
1 Corinthians 15:54-57

Your paraphrase:

For I am sure that neither death nor life, nor angels nor rulers, nor things present nor things to come, nor powers, nor height nor depth, nor anything else in all creation, will be able to separate us from the love of God in Christ Jesus our Lord.
Romans 8:38-39

Your paraphrase:

And [Jesus] said to him, "Truly, I say to you, today you will be with me in Paradise."
Luke 23:43

Your paraphrase:

For the righteous man is taken away from calamity; he enters into peace; they rest in their beds who walk in their uprightness.
Isaiah 57:1-2

Your paraphrase:

For if we live, we live to the Lord, and if we die, we die to the Lord. So then, whether we live or whether we die, we are the Lord's.
Romans 14:8

Your paraphrase:

He will wipe away every tear from their eyes, and death shall be no more, neither shall there be mourning, nor crying, nor pain anymore, for the former things have passed away."
Revelation 21:4

Your paraphrase:

A LITTLE STRONGER—The Bible proves to me God is stronger than death, so I will not live in fear. Death may be certain, but my eternal life with God is even more certain.

Frances Havergal, lived and moved in the Word of God. His Word was her constant companion. On the last day of her life, she asked a friend to read to her the 42nd chapter of Isaiah. When the friend read the sixth verse. "I the Lord have called thee in righteousness, and will hold thine hand, and will keep thee," Miss Havergal stopped her. She whispered, "Called—held—kept. I can go home on that!" And she did go home on that.[6]

There are Christians of a certain tribe in Africa who never say of their dead "who die in the Lord" that "they have departed." Speaking, as it were, from the vantage point of the Glory world, they triumphantly and joyously say, "They have arrived!"[7]

The French nurse who was present at the deathbed of Voltaire (French writer, intellectual and playwright who lived during the 1700's), was urged to attend an Englishman who was critically ill. She asked: "Is the man a Christian?" "Yes," came the reply, "He is a man who lives in the fear of God, but why do you ask?""Sir," she answered, "I was the nurse who attended Voltaire in his last illness, and for all the wealth of Europe, I would never see another infidel (unbeliever) die!"[8]

OH, FOR GRACE TO TRUST HIM MORE

My years on this earth have been short compared to saints with double my life span. But over my life, I've begun to see differences in the way believers face challenges, struggles, and bad news. I've always been intrigued by these differences, wondering, *If we are reading the same Bible, worshiping the same God, indwelt by the same Holy Spirit, and receiving the same promises and eternal home, then why do some fall into despair while others face each challenge with a stronger faith, a mightier courage, and a deeper optimism?*

Before I go on, what do you think? How can we all believe in the same God, yet only some live stronger when bad news comes?

Maybe you wrote some things like this:

- Some lack spiritual maturity.
- Some believe God's promises, but don't understand how to apply them to life or hard circumstances.
- Some forget to turn to God's promises, focusing only on their struggles.

I love the story of a difficult Christian woman. Her husband one day lamented, "I cannot imagine what she would be like if the Holy Spirit did not live in her and restrain all manner of malice that could come from her."

Maybe it's that way for some of us: with our natures not yet perfected, we are better than we have been because of the Holy Spirit, but not yet what we shall be. Not yet stronger when bad news comes.

Do you know someone who faced bad news with strength that obviously came from God?

What would happen if you called or emailed her to ask, "When you faced your bad news, how did God make you stronger, both at that very moment and then on your journey?"

One of my most vivid memories of strong faith during tragedy is of my dad. My younger sister drowned in the lake behind our house when I was fourteen. I was the one who found her. The next hour was a blur of prayers, paramedics, and so many people and their mighty efforts to save my sister. At last, the paramedics decided she could not be revived. They placed her sweet little body on the stretcher, but before they lifted her inside the ambulance, my daddy asked them if he could pray. I don't remember everything he said, but with all those around him holding hands, my daddy told the Lord he was humbly returning his daughter to her Heavenly Father. Daddy knew she was home with the Lord. He knew God was stronger than death and our overwhelming grief.

Years later, one of those paramedics contacted my dad. He told him he would never forget the day he prayed over his baby. The paramedic said he had never met a man with such strong faith. He was so curious about the God my dad prayed to, he went to church the next Sunday, where he eventually gave his heart and life to Jesus Christ.

Have you too seen an occasion when one believer's faith through a tragedy impacted others? If so, please describe the situation.

BEING MADE STRONGER

At the beginning of this week we talked about becoming stronger before bad news comes. My dad's trust in God gave him strength long before the day my sister died. On the day of her death, when his heart was crushed, the truth inside was revealed. What we all saw was a man who trusted God with his whole heart. Trust precedes strength. A fully surrendered trust allows the strength of God to be manifest in us.

That afternoon in July, I saw a God-given strength in my dad. He is a man I happen to adore, but he is just a man, nonetheless. The strength to face his bad news came not from himself, but from a heart fully surrendered to faith in God.

'TIS SO SWEET TO TRUST IN JESUS

Written by Louisa M. R. Stead, 1882

Louisa Stead's young husband died while trying to save a drowning child. In her grief, Stead penned the words to "'Tis So Sweet to Trust in Jesus."

Years later, Stead remarried and became a missionary. Her daughter Lily also entered the mission field. Stead's life was a testimony to the faithfulness of God.

The tragedy that prompted the lyrics of "'Tis So Sweet to Trust in Jesus" has resulted in bringing comfort to many souls for close to 130 years.

> 'Tis so sweet to trust in Jesus,
> Just to take Him at His Word;
> Just to rest upon His promise,
> And to know, "Thus saith the Lord!"
>
> Jesus, Jesus, how I trust Him!
> How I've proved Him o'er and o'er;
> Jesus, Jesus, precious Jesus!
> Oh, for grace to trust Him more.
>
> Oh, how sweet to trust in Jesus,
> Just to trust His cleansing blood;
> And in simple faith to plunge me '
> 'Neath the healing, cleansing flood!
>
> Yes, 'tis sweet to trust in Jesus,
> Just from sin and self to cease;
> Just from Jesus simply taking
> Life and rest, and joy and peace.
>
> I'm so glad I learned to trust Thee,
> Precious Jesus, Savior, Friend;
> And I know that Thou art with me,
> Wilt be with me to the end.

Read the following passages about trusting God. After each verse I've given you a place to note the benefit or gift God gives those who trust Him.

He is not afraid of bad news; his heart is firm, trusting in the Lord.
Psalm 112:7

The gift of trusting God:

Do not be afraid of sudden terror or of the ruin of the wicked, when it comes, for the Lord will be your confidence and will keep your foot from being caught.
Proverbs 3:25-26

The gift of trusting God:

Though an army encamp against me, my heart shall not fear; though war arise against me, yet I will be confident.
Psalm 27:3

The gift of trusting God:

You keep him in perfect peace whose mind is stayed on you, because he trusts in you. Trust in the LORD forever, for the LORD GOD is an everlasting rock.
Isaiah 26:3-4

The gift of trusting God:

FULLY SURRENDERED TO TRUST

When we trust Him, God makes us stronger. Where do you feel you are with regard to trusting? Make a mark somewhere on the line below.

●————————————————————————————————————●

Doubt keeps   Learning to trust   Leaning into trust   Fully surrendered to God
me from trusting God

As with most spiritual disciplines, learning to trust God takes practice. That means you begin to intentionally practice the action of trusting God with things you don't understand. If I were sitting with a friend who wanted to begin trusting God more, I might offer the following:

- At the very moment you realize you have an opportunity to trust God with what you don't understand, settle yourself to deal with God. Get alone if you can. Get down on your knees if you want. Tell the Lord you are intentionally choosing to trust Him.

- You really can tell God all the other feelings you're having. Doubt. Insecurity. Anxiousness. Whatever you're struggling with, I believe He longs for your honest conversation.

Review some of the Scriptures we have studied today and remember the gifts God gives to those who trust Him.

Sometimes when trusting is very difficult, I ask God for encouragement: "Lord, I know You don't have to, but would You send some kind of encouragement to me? My heart is so heavy and I just need something."

I can't tell you how many times God has answered a prayer like that with a song on the radio or a note in the mail or just a billboard I read driving down the road. When you ask God for an encouragement, make sure you lift up your eyes and look for His answer.

Determine to return to this place of prayer when you feel trust slipping away.

I hope you realize no formula substitutes for trusting God, but there is a way to begin. I always love asking a woman to learn to trust God because I have full confidence He will be faithful to bless her obedience.

As you practice the discipline of trusting God, you can almost feel spiritual strength begin to rise in your soul. Oh, how I pray for a new strength in you—the strength that comes to those who trust.

All his precepts are trustworthy.
Psalm 111:7

A LITTLE STRONGER—Facing my bad news with strength means asking God for the grace to trust Him more. I have decided it's time to learn how to trust Him more.

VIEWER GUIDE SESSION 4

PSALM 84
PASSING THROUGH BACA

Ephesians 2:8

GRACES THAT GOD GIVES THE TRAVELER ON THE JOURNEY

- We set our _____ to go toward God but, truly, we are only _____ to the One who set His heart on us _____.

- The _____ for us is that God doesn't leave us _____.

- The _____ that God has for us is that He keeps _____ and He keeps _____.

VALLEY OF BACA

- Valley of Baca also called the Valley of _____.

- It was a _____ _____ in the journey. It was a _____ _____ in the journey.

- The Lord—____ _____ ____ through Baca.

- The grace is that the Lord has already _____ what we _____— that He's already ahead of us in this really dark place.

- Dig through the _____ ____ _____. Dig deep into the treasure of the Lord until you receive from Him the _____ _____ that He promises for all who are in the season of Baca.

- When we are in the Valley of Baca and our souls are thirsty and we need the Lord, we dig until His _____ becomes ours and the graces that God has _____, He has _____.

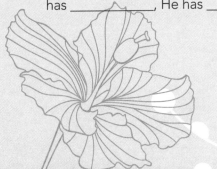

WEEK 4

GOD IS STRONGER THAN MY OVERWHELMING LIFE

DAY 1

TASK OVERLOAD

Have you ever been in a conversation with a girlfriend and suddenly find yourselves playing "My life is more overwhelming than your life"? What innocently begins as two friends sharing their schedules can quickly fall into the trap of task-overload comparison. Before you know it, you can subconsciously throw down the Top That card.

"How's your week looking?"

"Oh my goodness, I have no idea how I'm going to make it. My husband has meetings out of town, and on Tuesday night, each of the kids have games on different fields at the same time. It's insane."

"I hear you! My husband has been gone for two weeks, and the kids and I have been trading the sniffles. We feel lousy, but they can't really miss school and fall behind, so we've been spinning, trying to get it all done. I'm so far behind with my work. Plus, this week we have three soccer games, ballet practice, the mission night at church, and that huge biology project due."

"Wow, you're just as busy as I am! But with this broken leg I have, I'm trying not to let it slow me down. But getting from the wheelchair into the car—whew—it's tough."

I hope you're laughing. We've probably all done it. We compare our ridiculous schedules like it will help to just say it all out loud. Then somebody always throws down the Top My Broken Leg card. Ha!

When I'm operating in task overload, my schedule just spills out of me into my conversations.

Does that ever happen to you? How have you fallen into the comparison game?

Several years ago, I fell into this game one too many times. After those conversations ended, I realized I was downright depressed. I hadn't encouraged my friend one bit and now I had *my* schedule and *hers* in my head. Yuck. So I decided to stop.

I'm happy to listen to my friend's list of all she has to do, but I can skip my side of Top That. Actually, the comparison game is embarrassing to me. I want to do something about my task overload—something more significant than winning at the comparison game. I want to live differently and I bet you do too.

Several times in Scripture, we are told to examine our lives to see if we are living in accordance with the principles God has given. We find one such verse in Proverbs:

> The wisdom of the prudent [a person who is sensible and wise] is to discern his way.
> Proverbs 14:8 (definition added)

Are you living in a consistent state of task overload?

About five years ago, I examined my struggle, and yep, I was absolutely letting too much in. I woke up every morning with more to do than ten people could accomplish. My stomach ached constantly from the stress. On top of all that I had added pretending—pretending I could get it all done and could handle even more.

If you live in task overload, what have you added to make the burden even heavier?

Each one of us is in a different season of life. All of my children will have finished high school in four years and then our family's season will change. Our tasks will look different than they do today. But God has been clear to me about this season: He wants me to make some changes now instead of waiting.

Is God asking you to make some changes in this season of life?

Here are the two things God has been emphatic about with me:

- Responding to His direction for my life matters more than saying yes to all the people who might be disappointed.

- I am to kindly say no when opportunities clearly oppose God's direction to me for this season. I am to wait for His direction when I am unclear and give an enthusiastic yes when God says go.

Maybe God has already been speaking to you about this topic. What has He been saying?

A GODLY AND SCRIPTURAL NO

Some people are able to say no faster than their brain processes the options. They just always say no. It's easy for them. But the ability to say no to everything doesn't mean no is either godly or scriptural. We want to learn how to respond with no when it's God-led and Scripture-defined.

The co-author of *Boundaries,* Dr. John Townsend, once told me, "You don't say no just to be saying no. You say no when saying yes would hurt you. You say no when saying yes would be in opposition to God's leading and Scripture's principles."

Many in the Bible had to say no:
- Moses had to say no to his family to say yes to God's call to deliver Israel in Exodus 3.
- Ruth had to say no to her family and country to say yes to following Naomi to Bethlehem in Ruth 1.
- Nehemiah said no to serving King Artaxerxes so he could say yes to rebuilding the walls of Jerusalem in Nehemiah 1–2.
- The disciples said no to their families so they could say yes to following Jesus.
- Mary said no to her sister Martha to say yes to being with Jesus in Luke 10.
- And ultimately Jesus said no to the comfort of heaven so He could say yes to becoming our Savior.

Have you ever felt like it was "un-Christian" to say no? Do you realize that sometimes saying no is the most godly, scriptural way we can respond?

If God gave you permission to say no to some of the things currently overloading your life, would you have the courage to obey Him?

Stop for the next few minutes and spend some time in prayer. You may not hear from God immediately, but begin to pray about the task overload in your life. Is God asking you to say no to anything? Is He directing you to make changes that will realign your life around His priorities?

Make some notes here if you like, but more important, just pray.

IN HIM

In my video teaching at the end of this week, I talk about living this life "in Him." The Bible says all the strength needed for every obstacle we will face was purchased for us by Christ on the cross. When you became a follower of Christ, you were placed "in Him." In Him is all and He is in all (Col. 3:11).

Everyday this week I want to plant reminders in your heart about living in Him. God's strength is in you because you are in Christ. In Him you can become stronger. And Christ in you is stronger than all that tries to overwhelm you. To paraphrase a beautiful verse,

> *Greater is He who is in you than anything you will ever have to face on this earth.*
> *1 John 4:4 (my version)*

This life is so overwhelming that we fall apart if we forget this powerful truth.

We are in Him. Be strengthened today with that promise.

A LITTLE STRONGER—God is stronger than all the people who want me to say yes. I am determined to stay focused on Him, listening to Him, led by Him, living in Him, learning to graciously and kindly say no.

ALL THOSE DISTRACTIONS

Since the beginning of time, human beings have faced distractions. Right off the bat, Adam and Eve were so distracted by the forbidden fruit, they forgot about their relationship with God.

Distractions pull you away from more important things that need your focus.

I love people so much, I have always been easily distracted. But with the onset of mind-boggling, warp-speed technology, the distractions have multiplied like bunnies. *So many* distractions lurk at every turn.

For me, there are two kinds of distractions: (1) the ones I cannot control and (2) the ones I can learn to control.

Distractions I cannot control include the following:

- my 15-year-old daughter deciding she wants to talk to me about something important right in the middle of a good run of writing
- the garage door breaking to pieces (this morning) right when I'm driving out of town
- my dad texting to say he's on his way over
- a crying child running into the house for a bandage and a hug

What current distractions are beyond your control?

Part of my problem is I'm not really bothered by distractions. I want my life to be flexible enough to spend time with the people I love, care for my family, and care for our home when the inevitable next malfunction happens.

But a category of distractions has crept into my life these last years and begun to create mental and emotional chaos. I call them distractions I can learn to control:

- social media—Facebook, Twitter, Pinterest, Instagram, etc.
- ongoing, up-to-the-minute national and international news

- the ability to buy almost anything twenty-four hours a day (book a flight, buy a chandelier on eBay, anything)
- access to instant information and education (If I wonder, "Where in the world is Mayotte?" because my new friend has a netball tournament there, I can look it up [Indian Ocean, south of Seychelles, in case you were about to be distracted].)
- email

How about you? What are the distractions you can learn to control?

Consider the following verse:

But Martha was distracted with much serving.
Luke 10:40

To get the backstory for this passage, read about Mary, Martha, and Jesus in Luke 10:38-42. Martha was the distracted one. Mary had chosen the "good portion."

Have you ever been distracted from what really matters because you were doing and serving?

SET LIKE A FLINT

Along with the call to be a faithful follower, there are a few things I am absolutely sure the Lord has called me to do. Love my husband. Love my children. Serve, bless, and provide for my family. Teach the Bible. Use my life to point everyone I meet to Jesus.

Two passages in Scripture give me direction for my assignment:

And whatever you do, in word or deed, do everything in the name of the
Lord Jesus.
Colossians 3:17

Whatever your hand finds to do, do it with your might.
Ecclesiastes 9:10

I believe the Scriptures are clear. I am supposed to give these callings my best work. And I want to. With all my heart, I long to do all God has called me to do with all my might for His glory.

But the distractions—those stinky, frustrating distractions. They pull me away and waste my time and make me forget what matters more. Their allure is powerful, but God is stronger than all your distractions. Read the words of Isaiah:

> But the Lord GOD helps me; therefore I have not been disgraced; therefore I have set my face like a flint.
> Isaiah 50:7

Oh, how it gives me peace to hear the prophet declare, "God helps me." Because I really need His help. I long for His help. I am learning that I must turn to Him for help, because the next part of this verse is my desire—to set my face like a flint. Essentially, I need God's help to not be distracted from what He has called me to do. I need His help to set my face like a flint. To determine that I will not give way to lesser things. Lesser pursuits.

I truly believe God allows a time to enjoy the trivial, the silly, and the ancillary. But not when it distracts me from my calling. And there, my friends, is my trouble. I must ask God for His help. He is stronger than the allure of distraction. I must call on Him where I have not been strong.

What would it mean to set your face like flint concerning the distractions you could learn to control?

God assigned the prophet Nehemiah the task of rebuilding the walls of Jerusalem. Nehemiah undertook his work with focus and passion. Several times, people asked him to come down from the wall and talk to them. His reply? "I am doing a great work and I cannot come down" (Neh. 6:3).

Last week, I was moaning to a sweet friend because of my increasing stack of unanswered emails. She redirected me to this passage and firmly reminded me, "You are completing God's assignment to you. Answering email would be a distraction. You are up on the wall and cannot come down until it's done."

Luke 9:51 says that Jesus "set his face to go to Jerusalem." Determined to complete His assignment on earth, Jesus stayed focused "for the joy that was set before Him" (Heb. 12:2). Jesus knew where He had come from (heaven) and where He would return after His life was done (heaven). The promise of what was before Him kept His face set on His task.

He can help. He wants your life and mine to be spent on greater things, not wasted with trivial things. If you ask God to be stronger than your distractions, I believe He will answer. Let's end today by asking God for His help. Let's pray and listen for God's answer.

Below, list the distractions you need God to help you overcome. Then write what you are hearing God say.

My distractions	God's help

The distractions I can learn to control will require a new discipline. A new victory. A new strength. If you've just found Pinterest, or love to know what's going on in the world, or feel tied to your email, you may need a new strength to confront new distractions.

The Lord has given me help by giving me the desire to keep my life in order. I truly want to do everything He has called me to do for His glory. For me, that means my callings come first. Fun distractions are for later. I've had the equation backward too many days. Maybe you have too. And honestly, I'm just like you. I have to wake up every single day and remember the order.

God's assignments to me come first.

The fun, silly distractions can come later.

A LITTLE STRONGER—God is stronger than all these distractions, so I'll ask Him to help me everyday. My goal is to set my face like a flint on the calling He has given me.

UNREALISTIC EXPECTATIONS— MINE AND THEIRS

Repeat after me: Only God is perfect.

I am not.

They are not.

This world is not.

Only God is perfect.

Only God is perfect.

Somewhere in my dreams, I drew myself living inside the pages of a magazine. The house is not only clean, it's styled, organized, and accessorized. Candles are lit. Soothing music plays. My children are clean and smiling and doing chores no one ever asked them to do. My husband is happy, rested, and just finished playing eighteen holes of golf. My friends are not disappointed with me because I can talk on the phone for hours, meet them for lunch anytime, and run away for a girls weekend whenever they'd like. A cool breeze wafts through open windows, making us feel fresh and alive. Sweet, bug-free roses bloom outside. The dogs never bark at strangers walking by. My body feels strong and healthy. I am smart. I am able. I can do anything.

Do you have a magazine dream? If so, what would it look like?

If you are anything like me, most of my dreams include almost perfect people and almost perfect places and almost perfect relationships. I expect a bump or two along the way, but bumps could be resolved with the speed of a television sitcom—thirty minutes of smart conversation, ending with hugs and smiles.

Does any of this resemble dreams you have had or still hold onto?

If we take all our dreamy, unrealistic expectations and add the unrealistic expectations from the people we love, we create a dangerous concoction: a recipe for an overwhelming, disappointing life. After all, burnout comes not from work, but from not achieving expectations.

Maybe we should repeat our beginning truth again: only God is perfect.

LETTING EVERYONE OFF THE HOOK

I am praying that today will be the day we let the world, the people we love, and ourselves off the hook. Do you believe God can make you strong enough to do that? He can and even better, I believe He will.

First, just a few verses to underscore that only God is perfect:

> *For I will proclaim the name of the LORD; ascribe greatness to our God! The Rock, his work is perfect, for all his ways are justice. A God of faithfulness and without iniquity, just and upright is he.*
> *Deuteronomy 32:3-4*

> *This God—his way is perfect.*
> *Psalm 18:30*

> *The law of the LORD is perfect.*
> *Psalm 19:7*

It bears repeating as many times as you need to hear it: only God is perfect.

Have you expected someone or something other than God to live up to your expectations? To fill you up? To make you whole? To always keep his/her promise? To respond to your parenting with kind obedience? To be your Savior?

They can't. They were not created to complete you. To fill you. To save you.

Have you expected too much of yourself—to be the best mom, best daughter, best wife, best student, best friend, best employee, best follower of Christ?

Disappointment happens when reality doesn't meet expectations.

You can't. From the first breath you drew, you have needed a Savior. You are imperfect and flawed.

You will be disappointed on this earth and you will also disappoint others who expect unrealistic things from you.

What if God gave you the grace to be free from unrealistic expectations—theirs and yours. Romans 12 says the power to transform (to change) happens when our mind is renewed.

> *Be transformed by the renewal of your mind.*
> *Romans 12:2*

In today's study, renewal of your mind means a renewed focus on the only One who is perfect and a renewed understanding of our flaws and our great need for a Savior. Hebrews 7:11 says:

> *Now if perfection had been attainable through the Levitical priesthood (for under it the people received the law), what further need would there have been for another priest to arise after the order of Melchizedek, rather than one named after the order of Aaron?*

Essentially, if we could have been perfect, Jesus would not have needed to come as our High Priest. But we have proven time and again that we need a Savior. Jesus had to come because perfection has never been attainable. Let your mind be renewed. Perfection is not ours. Only God is perfect. Let your mind be renewed. You need a Savior and everyone you love does too.

Just take a minute here for a prayer of gratefulness. Jesus took you off the hook when He died on the cross. He bore our sin and imperfection. You do not have to be what you can never be. I do not have to be what I can never be. Oh, hallelujah.

Use this space to write a prayer of praise if, like me, writing sometimes helps you say things better:

Every time I expect myself or someone or something to be what only Christ can be, I have built an unrealistic expectation sure to disappoint. But by grace, Jesus Himself can make you strong enough to lay down unrealistic expectations. He is stronger than our imperfection and He will make you strong enough to accept our flawed reality. We all need a Savior. Only God is perfect.

So let's do this. Who needs to be let off your hook today? Your husband? A wayward child? You and your high expectations? Write their names in the space below.

Now make this declaration for each name you have written:

_____, *you are off the hook.*

I kneel at the cross and lay down my unrealistic expectations about you. You are a human being who needs a Savior. Only God is perfect. I hereby release you from ever having to be my Savior, my fulfillment, and my joy. All that I need is in Him. Jesus Christ is my Savior. I am humbled and I am grateful.

To be able to live peaceably with hard and perverse persons, or with the disorderly, or with such as go contrary to us, is a great grace. —Thomas à Kempis

LIVING FREE

I am praying and anticipating the *clink, clink* sound of hooks falling all around us. I wish I could adequately describe the freedom that will come to your soul when you lay them all down. What has been heavy will be gone. What you have received, you will long to give.

We are free from God's holy expectation of perfection by His grace, because of His Son, Jesus.

We give to others what we have been given. By grace, they are off the hook with us. Our unrealistic expectations are laid at the cross.

Then we live in the freedom bought by grace, held by grace, and promised because of grace.

My heart is eager for you to live in the freedom of renewed focus on this truth—only God is perfect.

A LITTLE STRONGER—Only God is perfect. This truth renews my mind, so my life can be transformed. Today I will give what God has given me: grace for sin, grace for disappointment, and grace to release unrealistic expectations.

DAY 4

THE ILLUSION OF BALANCE

How many times have you heard someone say, "I'm just trying to find balance"? I used to say that all the time. Then it finally occurred to me that I was chasing an illusion. I'm not sure there will ever be balance in this world. Maybe there is external balance if you live in a monastery, or alone in a cave, or some place where living requires few external commitments.

But that is not the life God has given to me. Or called me to. Nor is it the life I desire. I love family and friends and laughter and purpose. I love serving and giving and becoming a different woman as I age. I love learning and changing and doing some things I've never done before. And when you are called to love lavishly and give generously, there just isn't going to be an external balance on this earth.

One glance at the best-selling success books shows readers around the world searching for balance. A four-hour work week. Margins. Mojo. Success in 18 minutes. You name it and there's a book to promise you can have it.

What about you? Have you been searching for an external life balance that seems elusive?

Do you long to live in a monastery or do you believe you're called to family and all the busyness required to care for the ones you love? Why?

The Bible doesn't promise us balance. In fact, the ministry of Jesus was full of overwhelming crowds, inconsistent disciples, judgmental, ever-present Pharisees, loneliness, and temptation. Jesus graciously came to live in our world where there were times of urgency and days with too many people. With all the demands of His day, Jesus lived with a consistent calm and wisdom. His soul was filled with grace and peace, and His daily activities were guided by an unwavering mission:

> *For the Son of Man came to seek and to save the lost.*
> *Luke 19:10*

Life all around Him was not balanced, but Jesus stayed steady and secure. He led with His inner life. Arranging external order was not His ambition. Living in obedience to the Father was the aim of His whole life.

When a balanced life becomes our quest, we are missing the message of the Scripture. The ambition of the Christian life is not balancing our things. The goal for the Christ follower is Christlikeness.

> *Therefore, as you received Christ Jesus the Lord, so walk in him, rooted and built up in him and established in the faith.*
> *Colossians 2:6-7*

> *Therefore be imitators of God, as beloved children. And walk in love, as Christ loved us and gave himself up for us.*
> *Ephesians 5:1-2*

When I look at the life of Christ, I realize I am not called to spend my life as a tightrope walker, tediously trying to keep all things in balance, searching for structure and control. By His goodness, I have been caught in a net called grace. Safe in that net, I am stronger in God's grasp than in all the empty promises balance tried to make. To be like Christ is my ambition. When I am more like Christ and less concerned with finding balance or success, then I respond to the demands of this world with His heart and His mind and His steady peace.

Show me a woman who is in over her head, yet responding to life with grace and peace, and I'll show you a woman who knows the stronger way. She has chosen to live like Christ.

We're going to spend the rest of today and tomorrow considering what it means to live more like Christ. He is stronger than your overwhelming life and He sent the Holy Spirit to provide His strength, so let's start there.

WE CAN BE LIKE HIM BECAUSE WE ARE IN HIM

Nobody wakes up one fine morning and just decides, "Today is the day I begin living like Christ." The desire to follow Christ and live like Him comes from the prodding of the Holy Spirit. The Holy Spirit draws us to God. The Holy Spirit shows us our great need of God. And then the Holy Spirit prompts us (some of us many, many times) to give our lives to Christ.

The Scriptures say we are "born again" when we turn away from our sin and turn to Christ to be saved from the penalty of our sin. Ephesians 2 says it this way:

You were dead in the trespasses and sins . . . But God, being rich in mercy, because of the great love with which he loved us, even when we were dead in our trespasses, made us alive together with Christ—by grace you have been saved.
Ephesians 2:1,4-5

When we live in sin apart from God, the Bible says we are living as dead people. When we turn to God for salvation, He makes us alive (born again), free from the penalty of sin, filled in our souls by the powerful presence of the Holy Spirit, and promised eternal life with Him. At salvation, we are relocated from death to life—from an orphanage into the family of God. From that day forward, our soul is forever hidden in Christ.

Now look at this:

And we all, with unveiled face, beholding the glory of the Lord, are being transformed into the same image from one degree of glory to another. For this comes from the Lord who is the Spirit.
2 Corinthians 3:18

By what power will our lives be transformed?

Can you transform yourself? Of course not, or you would have already done that!

Into whose likeness are you and I being transformed?

Yep, the Holy Spirit is the one who will transform us into the very image of the glory of the Lord.

But you will receive power when the Holy Spirit has come upon you.
Acts 1:8

At salvation the Holy Spirit brings the only power able to make us like Christ. That goes for you and me, but it also goes for the person you believe is so far away from God that she could never become like Christ. I've known a few people who tempted me to believe they were too far gone. But hold on, Sister: the power of God is bigger.

God's Spirit is big enough to transform your anxieties and fears. He has been big enough to give this broken woman a new confidence. He is bigger than our rejection, our arrogance, our very smart academic minds, and our ongoing sin that just keeps piling up.

Instead of rearranging our external schedules and commitments so they momentarily resemble something balanced, why don't you make a fresh commitment to cooperate with the Holy Spirit who longs to transform your inner being?

Christlikeness is the goal. We just forget it sometimes.

A LITTLE STRONGER—I will not keep searching for a balanced life in this overwhelming world. My ambition is to become like Christ, so that my inner being is strengthened to live as He lived.

DAY 5

LIVING IN HIM

Very simply, Jesus called His disciples with the words "Follow Me." He wanted them to walk as He walked. Talk as He talked. Imitate His behavior and attitude. Respond as He would respond.

Today, His call to us is the same: to have our inner being become more and more like Him, less and less like the women we were before we met Him—more and more like the women He designed us to be.

> *Whoever says he abides in him ought to walk in the same way in which he walked.*
> *1 John 2:6*

And while we're thinking about it, how's your walking in the same way going? In what ways do you look more like the image of Jesus this year than you ever have? Or has your walk looked about the same for a long time now?

I want to cover a lot of ground today, so I hope you won't mind if I pray and we jump in.

Father, please be powerfully present with my sister today. Engage her heart with these Scriptures. Make them come alive to her in a fresh, new way. Show her more than what's written on these pages. Teach us how to live every day in Christ. Until we are with Him and fully like Him, our hearts long to be transformed for Your glory. Amen and amen.

LIVING LIKE HIM

Imitating the character of Christ should become the most important pursuit in our lives. I can't think of a greater way to glorify God than by becoming more and more like Him. So right now I am praying these verses for all of us:

> *For this reason I bow my knees before the Father, from whom every family in heaven and on earth is named, that according to the riches of his glory he may grant you to be strengthened with power through his Spirit in your inner being.*
> *Ephesians 3:14-16*

The inner being is the place where we will become like Christ. Strengthened by the Holy Spirit, our character *can* become like His. To become like Him is the clear instruction of the Bible.

> Put off your old self, which belongs to your former manner of life and is corrupt through deceitful desires, and to be renewed in the spirit of your minds, and to put on the new self, created after the likeness of God in true righteousness and holiness.
> Ephesians 4:22-24

We cannot adequately cover all of the character of Christ in this study. That's why we spend a lifetime learning to be like Him. But for today, I want to give you some places to begin and encouragement from Scripture.

HOW CHRIST WALKED

Don't let the list below overwhelm you. Jesus was fully God, perfect in all His ways. We are His followers, longing to be like Him, only able because of the strength He provides. Can you let your inability to become anything even close to this list humble you and make you long for His power all the more?

After each of the character traits of Jesus, write a one-line prayer. Ask the Holy Spirit to increase your likeness to Christ in this area, but write something specific to where you are in life right now. I'll do one to get you started.

1. Jesus walked in holiness.

> But as he who called you is holy, you also be holy in all your conduct.
> 1 Peter 1:15

My prayer: God, I long to be like Christ in holiness, especially when the circumstance or situation doesn't seem very holy. Help me to bring holiness into moments like that, especially with my family, in private, when no one is looking.

Your prayer:

2. Jesus walked in obedience.

For as by the one man's disobedience the many were made sinners, so by the one man's obedience the many will be made righteous.
Romans 5:19

And by this we know that we have come to know him, if we keep his commandments. Whoever says "I know him" but does not keep his commandments is a liar, and the truth is not in him, but whoever keeps his word, in him truly the love of God is perfected. By this we may know that we are in him.
1 John 2:3-5

Your prayer:

3. Jesus walked in boldness.

And when Jesus finished these sayings, the crowds were astonished at his teaching, for he was teaching them as one who had authority, and not as their scribes.
Matthew 7:28-29

Your prayer:

4. Jesus walked in self-denial.

[Jesus] made himself of no reputation, and took upon him the form of a servant, and was made in the likeness of men.
Philippians 2:7 (KJV)

Your prayer:

5. Jesus walked in humility and service.

But whoever would be great among you must be your servant, and whoever would be first among you must be your slave, even as the Son of Man came not to be served but to serve, and to give his life as a ransom for many.
Matthew 20:26-28

Do nothing from selfish ambition or conceit, but in humility count others more significant than yourselves. Let each of you look not only to his own interests, but also to the interests of others.
Philippians 2:3-4

Your prayer:

6. Jesus walked in sacrifice.

For to this you have been called, because Christ also suffered for you, leaving you an example, so that you might follow in his steps.
1 Peter 2:21

Your prayer:

7. Jesus walked in tenderness.

Take my yoke upon you, and learn from me, for I am gentle and lowly in heart, and you will find rest for your souls. For my yoke is easy, and my burden is light.
Matthew 11:29-30

[Bear] with one another and, if one has a complaint against another, [forgive] each other; as the Lord has forgiven you, so you also must forgive.
Colossians 3:13

Your prayer:

8. Jesus walked in love.

Therefore be imitators of God, as beloved children. And walk in love, as Christ loved us and gave himself up for us, a fragrant offering and sacrifice to God.
Ephesians 5:1-2

Your prayer:

9. Jesus walked in patience.

But I received mercy for this reason, that in me, as the foremost, Jesus Christ might display his perfect patience as an example to those who were to believe in him for eternal life.
1 Timothy 1:16

Your prayer:

10. Jesus walked in devotion to prayer.

But he would withdraw to desolate places and pray.
Luke 5:16

Your prayer:

11. Jesus walked in delight.

[Look] to Jesus, the founder and perfecter of our faith, who for the joy that was set before him endured the cross, despising the shame, and is seated at the right hand of the throne of God.
Hebrews 12:2

Your prayer:

12. Jesus walked in contentment.

I have learned in whatever situation I am to be content. I know how to be brought low, and I know how to abound. In any and every circumstance, I have learned the secret of facing plenty and hunger, abundance and need. I can do all things through him who strengthens me.
Philippians 4:11-13

Your prayer:

Look back over your prayers. What treasures do you want to retain from these passages of Scripture and your time talking with God about them?

A LITTLE STRONGER—I set my heart on becoming more like Christ. I want it said of me, "She has become more like Jesus and He has made her stronger."

VIEWER GUIDE SESSION 5

PSALM 84

THE WORK AND THE JOY OF GOD'S STRENGTH

A woman is in _____ because she has believed in _____ as her _____.

The _____ _____ is Christ's representative in your _____, in your _____—the One who's coming to seal you with the truth that you _____ to the Lord.

The _____ teaches me that my _____ is a gift.

The _____ teaches me that my _____ to what God has called us to do is the fruit of Christ inside of me.

"The Christian life is gloriously difficult but the difficulty of it does not make us cave in. It rouses us up to overcome." —Oswald Chambers, *My Utmost for His Highest*

WEEK 5

GOD IS STRONGER THAN MY ATTITUDE

DAY 1

GOD OFFERS A NEW ATTITUDE

About an hour into writing today's study, I realized this week needs so much more than I can give. As I studied and outlined our days, my heart became increasingly heavy. Then a profound sense of urgency filled my heart. In these next days, the Bible verses we'll study have the power to rescue women from bondage, lead women out of darkness, and move believers from a shallow walk with Christ to a glorious depth.

I sent an email to my prayer team, asking them to pray for anointed writing and for you. Before the writing of these days has been finished, edited, printed, or shipped, we have prayed for you. And you have my commitment: I will continue to pray for you.

The fear that prompted my email and my prayers? I'm afraid you'll miss God's power this week. Afraid I'll get in the way of what God wants to do. Afraid we'll stay the same, when God has the power to make us stronger.

I'm grateful for righteous fear that sends me to my knees. So be advised, I think you may have to fight your greatest distractions this week. I know an evil one who does not want you to become stronger.

Will you take a few minutes on your knees too? And if you feel like you can, if the Holy Spirit gives you agreement, will you commit to allow God to deal mercifully and graciously with you this week? Let Him highlight some places you may have kept hidden? Will you commit to respond to His leading with your obedience? God can make us new women this week. Are you willing to commit to His compassionate, transforming work?

I, _____, am committed to all God has for me this week. I will respond in obedience. I will allow the Holy Spirit to work inside of me. I am surrendered to God.

We are going to spend five important days dealing with our attitude struggles, because we really have to confront this poison. Too many women have already fallen victim to toxic attitudes that destroy our joy, our peace, our contentment, and our hope. But, hallelujah, this soul poison has not left us without an antidote. The power of God is stronger.

YOUR ATTITUDE MATTERS

Proverbs 23:7 says, "For as he thinks within himself, so he is" (NASB).

Too many of us have become the women we think we are, instead of the women Christ declares we can be. Some give their heart to Jesus but refuse to put on the mind of Christ, retaining a bad attitude. By "bad attitude," I don't just mean grumpy. I mean defeated or arrogant or stuck or petty or you name it.

Write down some other attitudes that belong to the category of "bad."

Any time we choose to consistently live with an attitude different from the attitude of Jesus, it's just downright wrong, not to mention miserable and embarrassing.

Have you ever been tempted to give up on a woman with a bad attitude? I have. They can be so draining. And self-justifying. And stuck. And hopeless. If I hear one more woman rationalize her bad attitude by saying, "That's just the way God made me," or "That's just how I am," I think I might stand in my chair and start yelling Bible verses. Oops, is that a bad attitude? Sometimes I want to give up on a woman with a bad attitude. Until I remember that even a woman with a 40-year bad attitude is *not* bigger than my God. He. Is. Still. Stronger.

NEW NATURE, NEW ATTITUDE

At birth, we already possess a sin nature (Eph. 2:1-3), but when we believe in Christ, we are born again into His divine nature (2 Pet. 1:3-4). No longer do we have to live according to the nature we were born with (our flesh); because of Christ, we can live according to the Spirit.

Have you ever heard someone complain about babies and the terrible twos? As the mother of four babies, I decided it was actually the terrible eighteen months. None of my children ever waited until age two to cut loose with their craziness. It usually began about around eighteen months. Up until then I could have easily doubted the whole idea of a sin nature from birth. But with my own eyes, four different times, I witnessed the unveiling of our sin nature.

So, at eighteen months old, my children would begin acting like big, fat sinners. Temper tantrums. Lies. Jealousy. I didn't have to model any of those things. I had been with them every day of their eighteen months and not one of them had been lied to or treated with jealousy.

None of them had ever seen a squalling, foot-stomping, fist-swinging temper tantrum in their short little lives.

So I watched each unveiling with new theological understanding. What came inside us at birth finally works its way to the surface. No seminary professor ever has to convince me again. We are born with a sin nature. Four times I learned that lesson. Four times I have looked at the baby I loved more than life and declared, "You need a Savior."

Wayne Grudem writes:

> *A Christian should never say (for example), "This sin has defeated me. I give up. I have had a bad temper for thirty-seven years, and I will have one until the day I die, and people are just going to have to put up with me the way I am!" To say this is to say that sin has gained dominion. It is to allow sin to reign in our bodies. It is to admit defeat. It is to deny the truth of Scripture.*[1]

At the very moment of salvation, the bondage of sin is broken in your life. You are no longer enslaved by the old nature because salvation sets you free. The apostle Paul writes of the power salvation gives us over sin:

> So you also must consider yourselves dead to sin and alive to God in Christ Jesus . . . Sin will have no dominion over you, since you are not under law but under grace.
> Romans 6:11,14

In Christ, we have been given new power to overcome the old nature, the old patterns of sin, and the old attitudes. A sinful attitude cannot be our master after we come to Christ because Christians are dead to the ruling power of sin and alive to the new power to be changed.

I've alluded to this before, but in what ways were you dead before Christ made you alive?

I came to know Christ as a child, but I am still very much aware of places in my heart where sin could rule my life without Christ.

Jot down a few thoughts about your specific "dead" places.

To the Corinthians Paul wrote:

Therefore, if anyone is in Christ, he is a new creation. The old has passed away; behold, the new has come.
2 Corinthians 5:17

Because I never want another Christian woman to declare, "That's just my nature," let's nail down a little theology. When I take things step by step, sometimes I understand it better, so that's what we're going to do here. A very simple systematic theology (with Jesus Girl commentary) for understanding our new nature follows.

1. Long before you and I arrived on earth, Christ defeated sin on the cross. Before our need to be free of sin even happened, Jesus had already provided a way out. This makes me want to shout, "Thank You, Jesus!"

2. Every human being is born with a sin nature. From birth, you and I are enslaved by that nature—powerless and imprisoned. (I know, this is such a bummer. Go back and read number 1 for restored hope.)

3. At the moment of salvation, the chains of your sin nature are broken. The sin nature you were born with is exactly the one Christ defeated on the cross. His victory over sin is given (imputed, assigned, credited) to you when you believe. This means sin no longer has control over your nature. Believers still sin, but we no longer have to sin. I could not do it for myself, but Jesus set me free from my prison of sin.

4. At salvation, you are set free to grow as a new creation in Christ. You begin the journey of growing in holiness, becoming an imitator of Christ. Maybe you feel like you've been slow on the growing part, but today is a new day and God's fresh mercy keeps calling you up. Higher. Stronger. More like Him today than yesterday.

5. The rest of life on earth is the journey of spiritual growth called sanctification. As we grow in Christ, we can learn to more and more focus our minds on things of the Spirit. The old sin nature is still present but lacking its enslaving power. The growing Christian learns to turn away from old sin and take hold of the new power she has been given.

Well, my friend, right here is the very thing that could change everything. Growing. Learning. Turning.

Did God break the bondage of sin in your life a long time ago? If so, are you learning to live according to the Spirit who lives in you?

6. We will not be completely free of sin until heaven, but—thankfully—until then, we have the provision of God's grace and forgiveness in this ongoing battle against sin.

Insert your own happy dance here. Bless the Lord, oh my soul.

7. Once in heaven, the remnant of our sin will be removed. We will be, finally and fully, as God has promised. Home. Made new. Without stain or blemish. Redeemed for all eternity.

I just have no words. This truth sustains my soul.

> *Beloved, we are God's children now, and what we will be has not yet appeared; but we know that when he appears we shall be like him, because we shall see him as he is.*
> *1 John 3:2*

A LITTLE STRONGER—I will give God my struggle with my attitude. He alone has the power to make me new.

I THINK TOO MUCH OF MYSELF

How is your heart today? Still committed to an honest look at your attitude? Still willing to be transformed in ways God may direct? Don't forget: He is stronger than any thinking pattern or habit you have acquired.

Don't forget He is able to help you change. Don't forget He is merciful as He works. Our assignment is to remain willing.

> *Search me, O God, and know my heart! Try me and know my thoughts! And see if there be any grievous way in me, and lead me in the way everlasting! Psalm 139:23-24*

As a teenage girl, I was completely and totally obsessed with myself. If I had a conversation with a friend I wanted to impress, the moment the conversation ended, I would walk down the hall with all my insecurity and head straight into the bathroom to look into the mirror and check my hair or my acne.

Sadly (and embarrassingly), running to a mirror to see if I looked acceptable wasn't all. There were many more ways I thought too much of myself:

- I wouldn't leave the house unless I was just right. I constantly planned and replanned my hair, makeup, and clothes.
- I'd begin a note to a friend over and over, ripping the paper to shreds if I made a mistake, wrote too big or too little, or—heaven forbid—if I made a smudge.
- My life choices were meticulously planned in my head, each with one purpose in mind: me. My reputation. My accomplishments. My happiness.

I could write more examples, but I can't keep going. Besides, I think you get it.

My daughter is a teenage girl. She lives in my home and her cutie-pie friends are here all the time. I love them all. But interestingly, I see them struggle with the same temptation to hyper-self-focus. To this day, thinking about self too much continues to keep girls in bondage.

Did you struggle with an intense focus on yourself in your teenage years?

List some ways you have thought too much of yourself.

As we grow, we may change our responses and attitudes. As you read the following four responses, rate yourself by putting a percentage for how much each category represents your attitude.

___ *These girls become women who grow into maturity and stop thinking about self too much. They think about themselves to consider how they might grow, improve, and change. Each season of life brings new challenges, but they have not allowed self-centered "over-thinking" to control their minds.*

___ *These girls grow up to realize it's not socially or spiritually acceptable to continue with an intense self-focus, so they pretend something different on the outside, yet remain in bondage to their image, insecurities, and pain on the inside.*

___ *These girls grow up and believe the lie. They decide the struggle within is meant to be unleashed. As women, they freely flaunt the decision to only think of themselves. It seems funny when a woman calls herself a diva, unless she really is one.*

___ *These girls grow up believing a different lie called "My life should have turned out better than this." So they live hyper-focused on anger, regret, and what-ifs. They wrestle the demons of bitterness and resentment every day.*

Describe in a sentence or two how you have dealt with the self-focus that plagues us all.

How has self-focus changed through the years for you?

One woman might think about herself so much that she begins living with an entitled attitude. A different woman might live outwardly bitter or angry. Yet another can believe she is pretending enough to cover her self-focus, but the truth of her struggle always seeps out. Praise God that godly women show us examples of healthy thinking.

Mark any of the things below that might be a symptom of you thinking about yourself too much:

❏ *I am full of ambition. It drives me, even consumes me some days.*
❏ *I live in the past with my regrets and failures.*
❏ *I have lots to offer this world and I just want everyone to know.*
❏ *I live in the past, reliving my glory days and my accomplishments.*
❏ *I am a victim of crime or abuse or abandonment.*
❏ *I spend a lot of time wondering, What if _____?*
❏ *I have truly been done wrong, too many times, by too many people.*
❏ *I suffer daily with disease or disability.*
❏ *Nothing has ever gone right for me and I think about it a lot.*

HEALTHY THINKING ABOUT YOURSELF CAN PRODUCE

- a righteous confidence to do God's will
- a determination to pursue Christlikeness
- a holy ambition
- an awareness of your limitations and God's provision

UNHEALTHY THINKING ABOUT YOURSELF CAN PRODUCE

- bouts of mild to major depression
- reoccurring battles with misery, negativity, and unhappiness
- a nagging lack of contentment and peace
- a loss of joy and the ability to rejoice
- relationship struggles

Let me stop right here and say a couple of things. First, I am not a counselor. (Please visit *aacc .net* to find a Christian counselor near you. I've probably seen six different counselors and each has taught me how to apply God's Word faithfully to the struggles I have faced.) Second, at times, choosing survival or healing requires you to focus intently on yourself.

This very day, my daddy is filled with grief. His grief is right and healthy. His thoughts are mostly focused on his memories, his deep loss, and his yearning to have my mom back with him. I believe this time of being focused on self is necessary and good for him. But if years go by, and my dad continues to be focused on his grief, he could move from healthy grieving into greater struggles that might keep his attitude in bondage.

Do you see what I am saying? These few pages cannot adequately cover the scope of hurts and needs today's topic may open for you. Changing our attitudes may require so much more than one discussion, a prayer, and a decision. If you need attitude transformation, I'm praying you will stay with this until transformation has begun. Don't let yourself give up.

- We do yearn for what has been lost. We all rightfully wish for what might have been.
- Yes, most of us wish we could go back and do so many things differently.
- It's awful for anybody on this earth to suffer disease or disability or even the awful treatments intended to cure them.
- No woman on the planet should ever be abused or abandoned.
- For a lot of us, the old days really were better days and these days are full of heavy burdens.
- Assigned to live on a fallen planet, we will all experience grief, longing, and pain in our souls.
- This life is hard and times can get you down. But oh, hallelujah, God has provided a Savior, so what may wound us does not have to defeat us.

Healthy grief, ache, and memories can become unhealthy. When they do, the unhealthy struggle will launch a battle for your mind. And from that battle, your mind can produce an attitude with the power to shape your heart, your choices, and your countenance. The questions for the woman of God are these:

Will you ask God to reveal any place, big or small, where you retain unhealthy thinking and ask Him to begin to heal your mind?

Will you ask God for grace so that your spirit is willing to be changed?

DECIDING TO BE TRANSFORMED

Maybe you really do think about yourself too much. Join the club of billions. We've all wasted too much time with unhealthy thinking. But my prayer team is all over this with me, and we are asking God not to let you stay there. Read these instructions to us from His Word:

> *Do not be conformed to this world, but be transformed by the renewal of your mind . . . For by the grace given to me I say to everyone among you not to think of himself more highly than he ought to think, but to think with sober judgment, each according to the measure of faith that God has assigned.*
> *Romans 12:2-3*

Last night I couldn't sleep and in keeping with my middle-of-the-night ritual, I reached for my iPad, turned the brightness down low, and began reading the news. Sleep specialists tell you not to do this, but I promise, it really helps me fall back asleep. I somehow clicked my way to an article about a woman who decided to stop yelling at her kids for a year. This mother of four confessed she had been yelling every time something didn't go the way she wanted it to for years. Yelling was her habit. Yelling came from an attitude shaped by her self-focused mind.

One day a repairman was at her house. She forgot he was there and proceeded to lose it, as usual, with her children. Realizing this poor man had just witnessed her awful outburst completely embarrassed her. She decided that very day to stop yelling. So, cold turkey, the mom made one radical decision and just stopped. At the writing of the article, she had been 404 days without one tiny peep of a yell. As you can imagine, her new attitude had changed everything for good. Her heart. Her home. Her marriage. Her kids.

What would you write as a spiritual moral to the story of the woman who stopped yelling?

The woman I read about never mentioned one word about Jesus, so I have no idea about her faith. But that's not the point. The point is we do have Jesus! He lives in us. We have been given the power that can transform our lives.

Is God asking you to make a radical attitude decision? If you could stop thinking about yourself too much, what kind of woman do you think you could become?

A LITTLE STRONGER—I have mistakenly believed I must fill my mind with thoughts of myself—my dreams, hurts, improvement, happiness. But too much thinking has left me unhealthy. It's time to live stronger than this.

I THINK TOO LITTLE OF MYSELF

Do you ever have days when you feel like you are only as good as what the last person said to you? Hearing someone say, "Your hair looks really nice," has the power to boost your attitude. Just as easily, "I don't think red is your best color," can take you down. Tell us something good and we're good. Send a hint of negative and we're down. Or offended. Or sad.

Have you already lived too many days like that? Blown around by the winds of opinion and careless remarks? Do you sometimes feel like you're riding an emotional roller coaster, wondering why are you easily moved from one emotional place to another?

When thinking too little of ourselves becomes unhealthy, we may have done some of the following things:

- forgotten we belong to God and our value has been given to us by Him
- listened to the voice of the accuser and believed his lies about us
- given other people the power to speak for God
- misunderstood biblical humility
- lived according to our feelings, lacking wisdom and forsaking our trust in God

What other ways have you seen women live unhealthy lives because they think too little of themselves?

When thinking little of yourself is healthy and biblical, it can produce beneficial effects:

- a godly humility
- an ability to recognize and serve the needs of others
- an others-centeredness and generosity
- a life surrendered to God's glory

I have often forgotten who I became the day I gave my life to Jesus. This world can be unrelenting with its wounding. Sometimes it feels like the pain will never end and the rejection might go on forever.

In the years of my divorce, I was so broken and my heart so bruised, the voice of the accuser was almost all I could hear. The more he yelled into my soul, the more I forgot who I was. The louder he became, the less I became.

Through the years, his lies seemed to be winning. *Maybe I deserve everything I am getting. Maybe my brokenness is too great for God to heal. What if I am an abomination to God? What if God can't have anything to do with a woman like me?*

As the lies became greater, I became smaller. My confidence was crushed by my shame. My countenance was fragile and fearful, always clinched, preparing for the next emotional ambush. My dreams had completely evaporated. After years in that kind of darkness, with a spiritual attack that would not subside, the hope that remained inside of me shrank to a tiny thread, thin and frayed, barely visible, some days almost gone.

Twelve years later I still cry as I type those last two paragraphs. I just had to stop and walk away. Let the tears fall again. Grieve. Wash my face. It still hurts so bad to remember what Satan did to me.

Wrapped up in his lies, I learned how to think too little of myself. The accuser almost had me, except for one thing: I still belonged to God. I was His, but I had forgotten my name, address, and number.

NAME, ADDRESS, AND NUMBER

Most of the women I meet who think too little of themselves have also forgotten their name, address, and number. Maybe you have sometimes forgotten too. Write your name in each blank below.

Your Name: Beloved, Child of God

> *See what kind of love the Father has given to us, that we should be called children of God; and so we are. The reason why the world does not know us is that it did not know him. Beloved, we are God's children now.*
> *1 John 3:1-2*

_____, *you are the beloved child of God. The accuser may descend on you. His lies may paralyze you. Shame may overwhelm you. But he cannot ever have you. You belong to God.*

What practical difference might remembering your name make?

Your Address: Citizen of Heaven

> *But our citizenship is in heaven.*
> *Philippians 3:20*

_____, *your address is in heaven. This world doesn't feel like it fits sometimes, because it's not your home. You were made for more and your soul longs for where it was made to be.*

What practical difference might reminding yourself of your citizenship make?

Your Number: One in Christ Jesus

> *For as many of you as were baptized into Christ have put on Christ. There is neither Jew nor Greek, there is neither slave nor free, there is no male and female, for you are all one in Christ Jesus.*
> *Galatians 3:27-28*

_____, *you are one in Christ Jesus. There are no categories or divisions with God. No social standings. No upper class or lower class or people who live on the wrong side of the tracks.*

What practical difference might remembering your number make?

After Paul reminds the Philippians of their address, he encourages them.

> *Therefore, my brothers, whom I love and long for, my joy and crown, stand firm thus in the Lord, my beloved.*
> *Philippians 4:1*

Belonging to God is stronger than every lie Satan uses to make you think little of yourself. You and I are called to stand firm in the truth that makes us stronger.

The next time you feel little, remember your name, your address, and your number.

God gave us instructions for remembering in Deuteronomy 6. I love the visual pictures in this passage. Maybe this will help you remember too.

> You shall love the Lord your God with all your heart and with all your soul and with all your might. And these words that I command you today shall be on your heart. You shall teach them diligently to your children, and shall talk of them when you sit in your house, and when you walk by the way, and when you lie down, and when you rise. You shall bind them as a sign on your hand, and they shall be as frontlets between your eyes. You shall write them on the doorposts of your house and on your gates.
> Deuteronomy 6:5-9

And then, so very aware of our humanity, God adds,

> Take care lest you forget the LORD.
> Deuteronomy 6:12

A LITTLE STRONGER—As long as I remember my name, address, and number, Satan cannot make me feel little.

I JUST WANT EVERYONE TO LOVE ME

Before I went to bed last night, I clicked on my outline for today's study. I've found if I glance at my next day of writing, my heart has time to become reacquainted with the topic. Through the night and the next morning, I can pray and think. By the time I sit down to write, I still may not know what to do, but at least I'm prepared for what's coming.

One little peep at today's outline and I realized, *Well, shoot, I guess it's my turn*. Sometime in the night, I felt the nudge of God's grace and my heart surrendered. If the Lord wills it, I want Him to remove the thin veil that hides my struggle. If it will help somebody, then let them see.

So here you go. I, Angela, have spent most of my life just wanting everyone to love me. From that very unhealthy place, I have suffered many wounds and wasted many years, not to mention all the opportunities I've missed while chasing acceptance and love.

Anybody else want to join me here?
_____ Yep, I have belonged to the "just love me" club too.
_____ No way, I ditched that nonsense a long time ago.

For those of you who checked "No way," I should warn you in advance, the rest of us are going to need a little grace from you. We have wanted some of your strength for a very long time.

THE PATH CALLED PLEASING

They have a name for people who just want everybody to love them: pleasers. In case you haven't heard, the pleasing path is a dead-end street. You just can't please some people enough, some never at all, and still others will manipulate, tease, and even abuse the pleaser in us. The pleaser lives an exhausted and exhausting life.

Intellectually, I have known being a pleaser was a bad way to go, but somehow I just couldn't find the way to change. Truth is, I just wanted everyone to love me even after I understood my attitude was unhealthy. Even when I knew better, I still struggled. And, yes, in case you're wondering, I did read the book called *Boundaries*. Bought it. Read it. Discussed it. A few years later, co-author John Townsend and I had a huge conversation about this very struggle. I knew I was unhealthy.

As the self-appointed pleaser spokeswoman, I can tell you a little more about our kind. Most of us pleasers are insecure, weak-kneed people. We might talk a big talk sometimes, but at the end of the day, we will stand on our heads, juggling flaming arrows if we think it might make someone happy, especially someone who is perpetually unhappy or continually requiring more of us than we can give. We are conflict-avoidant, risk-adverse, work-ourselves-into-oblivion, easily pushed, easily bullied, big-chicken kind of people.

As Christian women, we can hide our true motives (wanting everyone to love us) and label our misguided efforts as "our spiritual acts of service."

Do you think two women could do the exact same act with different motives—one with a healthy desire to serve and the other with a pathological need to please?

If so, how can we discern the difference in our own motivations?

So why in the world do pleasers continue to want everybody to love them even after they have been intellectually and emotionally convinced it's unhealthy? I bet there are several million reasons, but I'm going to sum up the ones I'm most familiar with.

1. We have not fully understood God's love for us.

2. We have not fully understood what Christ did for us on the cross.

3. Without understanding, we continue in spiritual darkness. We keep trying to do for ourselves what Christ has already done for us: acquire love and acceptance.

Why do women struggle with wanting to be loved by everybody?
1.

2.

3.

Because of Christ's finished work, Christians already possess the approval, the love, the security, the freedom, the meaning, the purpose, the protection, the new beginning, the cleansing, the forgiveness, the righteousness, and the rescue we intensely long for and, in fact, look for in a thousand things smaller than Jesus every day—things transient, things incapable of delivering the goods.[2]

—Tullian Tchividjian

Fourteen or so years ago, I was profoundly impacted by *The Call* by Os Guinness. Slow and steady, I read words so fresh and new to me. When I had finished, I declared with all my heart, *God is the audience of One. My life's ambition is to please Him alone.*

Truly, my heart's intent and desire was to live fully satisfied in God's love for me. A life that "danced" for Him alone. He was the One I longed to please. I desperately longed to be different, but sadly, my pleaser attitude did not begin to change until I began to more fully understand who I was in Christ.

I'm going to do that step-by-step theology thing again. It helps me think logically, so I'm hoping it helps you too.

- On the cross, Jesus earned God's full approval, acceptance, and affection for us. If the cross didn't make God happy, you're not going to make Him happy.

- We have not understood the full extent of what Christ has accomplished. Read the Book of Colossians for starters.

- Christ's accomplished work on the cross can be life-changing revelation for pleaser-girls. We are free!

- Because Jesus earned all of God's love and acceptance for us, we no longer require another love to become approved, valuable, or worthy.

- We can live fully and intentionally before an audience of One, our Father in heaven.

- We do not have to live in the stress and dysfunction of trying to win everybody's love, because we have already been given all the love our heart craves in Jesus.

We have not ceased to pray for you, asking that you may be filled with the knowledge of his will in all spiritual wisdom and understanding.
Colossians 1:9

Paul prays for his readers to be filled with the knowledge of Christ's work for them. The implication is that we can be *filled*. We can grasp the fullness of this great truth and it can change us.

Would you describe yourself as having been filled with the knowledge of God's love for you? Why or why not?

May you be strengthened with all power, according to his glorious might, for all endurance and patience with joy, giving thanks to the Father, who has qualified you to share in the inheritance of the saints in light.
Colossians 1:11-12

Paul says that in Christ, we have been qualified. Done. Finished. You have been qualified before the highest authority in the universe, the Creator. *Striving. Is. Done.* Not only have we been accepted, we have been crowned, blessed, and brought into the family. So why would we continue to strive for lesser credentials? Why would we beg for the fleeting love of anyone else when we have already received the full love and approval of the One Who Matters Most? I believe most of us continue to strive because we have not fully understood what this means.

Much of the Book of Colossians is devoted to our understanding the following:

- The fullness of God dwells in Christ (1:19).
- Believers are filled in Him (2:10).
- For those who belong to Him, Christ is all and in all (3:11).

Thus the fullness of God's love in us supplies all that our soul requires to be full. No one, no thing, and no accomplishment can fill our souls. That fullness comes in Christ alone. Just as important: no rejection, no unrequited love, no disappointment, and no demotion can diminish your value or your acceptance. Your full approval came in Christ and it cannot be removed by human hands, pink slips, tweets, or even loneliness.

To love and be loved on this earth is a gift from God. This kind of love comes through a variety of different relationships. This kind of love is a blessing to be treasured and enjoyed. Love becomes unhealthy when we must have it from everybody or anybody to feel approved and valued.

If you became a woman who lives in the full assurance of God's approval and acceptance, what would change about you? Take as long as you need here. I'll get you started . . .

Changes in my soul:

I could live at peace.

Changes in my home:

Changes in my relationships:

Practical, everyday changes:

Do you remember Day 1 of this week? I am still praying for our hearts to be open. God may be calling you to something radical and transforming. If you hear Him today, do not let your heart be hard.

> *For am I now seeking the approval of man, or of God? Or am I trying to please man? If I were still trying to please man, I would not be a servant of Christ.*
> *Galatians 1:10*

A LITTLE STRONGER—Every day, I will choose to live in the fullness of what Christ has done for me. I am fully approved. Fully accepted. Fully loved. No other approval is required or needed.

I JUST WANT EVERYONE TO LEAVE ME ALONE

After I was married to Scott, my children and I moved to the town where he lived, which was also the town where I had grown up. It had been more than twenty-five years since I had lived in Greensboro, North Carolina, so I was excited to come back and rekindle many sweet friendships. One of our first reconnections was a family dinner with John and Janet Funderburk, the couple who led my youth group.

Over dinner, we laughed about things my kids did and trips when their mom learned to snow ski. But eventually, John looked across the table and said from his big heart, "We sure have missed you, Angela. Somehow we just lost touch for too many years."

"Oh, John," I replied. "It wasn't you. It was me. I hid for a lot of years, so embarrassed about my divorce. I didn't know what to say to people, so I stopped responding. You may have lost track of me, but I didn't want to be found."

For many years, I was embarrassed and afraid of more judgment, so I just wanted everybody to leave me alone.

For what other reasons do women pull back, hide, and want everyone to leave them alone?

Wounded, broken women cross their arms, shut their doors, and turn people away. Maybe they're angry or maybe they're embarrassed or maybe they're trying to cover some crazy sin. But I'm pretty sure underneath it all is a wound that has never been healed.

THE HOUND OF HEAVEN

One of the things I love about the Lord is that He never stops pursuing you. You may close your heart and close your mind and close yourself off from His love, but He keeps coming after you. He is not deterred by grumpy women or locked doors. His love is stronger than the one who just wants everyone to leave her alone.

In 1893, Francis Thompson published a poem called "The Hound of Heaven," which begins like this:

> I fled Him, down the nights and down the days;
> I fled Him, down the arches of the years;
> I fled Him, down the labyrinthine ways
> Of my own mind; and in the mist of tears
> I hid from Him and under running laughter
> Up vistaed hopes I sped;
> And shot, precipitated,
> Adown Titanic glooms of chasmed fears,
> From those strong Feet that followed, followed after.[3]

The poem's style is more Victorian than most of us are accustomed to, but the image of our loving God relentlessly pursuing those who run and hide is so very powerful.

Pain rightfully makes us want to withdraw. Just as we yank our hand from a hot stove, the soul instinctively runs from the threat of more pain. Or more embarrassment. Or more shame. We find hiding places that make us feel safe. And we stand behind a bolted door, waiting silently for the ones who knock to just go away. Eventually, if you hide long enough, most of them do.

Except One.

He keeps coming after you because He knows He can heal your wounds. He knows He can keep you safe. He knows He is stronger than your fears. He knows He made you for more.

He made you for His love, and He made you to be loved by others. Read the prayer the apostle Paul prayed for you and me:

I love this beautiful description of God's love based on Ephesians 3:18 and John 3:16:

The Breadth—For God so loved the world

The Length—that He gave His only Son

The Depth—that whoever believes in Him should not perish

The Height—but have eternal life.

For this reason I bow my knees before the Father, from whom every family in heaven and on earth is named, that according to the riches of his glory he may grant you to be strengthened with power through his Spirit in your inner being, so that Christ may dwell in your hearts through faith—that you, being rooted and grounded in love, may have strength to comprehend with all the saints what is the breadth and length and height and depth, and to know the love of Christ that surpasses knowledge, that you may be filled with all the fullness of God.
Ephesians 3:14-19

What does Paul pray for us to have the strength to comprehend?

What measure of knowledge does he want us to have about what we shall comprehend?

Here's what I want you to know more than anything: the love of God never stops pursuing us. He keeps knocking on the door even when we stand silent on the other side. Even when we spit and scream and cry, His love never fails. He is the Hound of Heaven.

MADE FOR MORE

What I have learned about getting everybody to leave me alone is, if you reject them long enough and loud enough, people will eventually leave you alone. But God never does.

You see, God made us for His love, but He also made us for the love of others. When I began to understand more fully the faithfulness of this God who can heal my wounds and keep me safe, then I also realized He often uses other people to be part of His healing and safety to me. All through the New Testament we see instructions like these:

Love one another (John 15:12).
Bear one another's burdens (Galatians 6:2).
Do not neglect meeting together (Hebrews 10:24-25).
They devoted themselves to the apostle's teaching and fellowship (Acts 2:42).
We, though many, are one body in Christ (Romans 12:4).
Encourage the fainthearted, help the weak, be patient with them all
(1 Thessalonians 5:14).

God used a community of friends, family, and believers to coax me out of hiding so they could become part of His healing me.

How have you seen God use His people to heal and love the wounded?

Maybe you have felt like yelling at the world, "I just want everybody to leave me alone!" I hear you. I understand how life can make you feel that way. But I want you to know this: God made you for so much more. He made you for His love. He has made you to give and receive love from others.

Maybe the people who were supposed to love you have instead wounded you deeply. Maybe the trust you gave in the past was broken and abused. I want you to know how very sorry I am for every place of pain you have known. More important, I want to ask if you'd be willing to let God show you His faithfulness and the depth of His love. Have you felt the Hound of Heaven pursuing you? Would you be willing to let Him catch you today?

Show Him your wounds.

Tell Him your fears.

Let your heart begin to feel the breadth, length, height, and depth of His love.

Whisper to Him these words, *I want the more for which I am made.*

Can I pray for you?

God, there isn't a woman who doesn't want to run and hide at times. But thank You for always coming after us. Thank You for Your faithfulness, even when we have been far away. Today, please keep being our Pursuer, our Rescuer, and our Redeemer. Keep knocking on the doors we have locked. Today, I pray this sweet friend will trust Your goodness. I pray she will open locked places. May this be the day everything changes.

Because Jesus is our Savior, and He is stronger. Amen and amen.

A LITTLE STRONGER—My hurt makes me want to hide. Hiding and closing off everyone with my attitude is not what I desire. God has told me in a thousand ways that He loves me. Today I will let His love begin to change me.

VIEWER GUIDE SESSION 6

PSALM 84

MADE STRONGER TO LIVE WITH PASSION

Hebrews 12:1

What would it look like if I were to live in the strength that God provides—a passionate life?

- We are _____ by a great cloud of witnesses.

- Lay aside _____ weight.

- Avoid _____. Discouragement will hinder a passionate life.

- Center yourself on the _____ of the gospel.

- Fight to stay in the _____ of the Lord.

- Turn from your _____.

- You have to _____ through it to get to _____.

- Do not let yourself be _____ in their sin.

- Run with _____.

GOD IS STRONGER THAN EVERY BROKEN THING IN ME

MY BROKEN RELATIONSHIPS

Let's pray together as we begin this new week.

Father, thank You for all the lessons You keep giving to me about Your strength. I am learning so much about Your goodness and Your grace. Your strength for every place I am weak. Today, I give You my full attention. Make me stronger. In Jesus name. Amen.

I have my own journey, but everyone I meet has been touched by at least one broken relationship. You know the stories:

- children who haven't spoken to a parent in years
- siblings who went their separate ways
- lost boyfriends
- divorced husbands
- broken friendships
- isolated neighbors

God can heal a broken heart, but He has to have all the pieces.

> *My son, give me your heart, and let your eyes observe my ways.*
> Proverbs 23:26

We must acknowledge that sometimes a relationship has to be severed, especially if it has become toxic, abusive, criminal, and destructive. Proverbs has a word for the kind of people who can be harmful to us—*fool*—and gives us many emphatic and direct instructions for dealing with fools. Here are just a few:

> *Leave the presence of a fool, for there you do not meet words of knowledge.*
> Proverbs 14:7

> *Whoever walks with the wise becomes wise, but the companion of fools will suffer harm.*
> Proverbs 13:20

Do not speak in the hearing of a fool, for he will despise the good sense of your words.
Proverbs 23:9

Answer not a fool according to his folly, lest you be like him yourself.
Proverbs 26:4

Why do you suppose Proverbs says so much about relationships with fools?

Summarize in one sentence the teaching of the Scriptures you just read.

Sometimes our broken relationships involve the healthy decision to leave the presence of a fool. But even those right decisions are not without the accompanying pain and scars left in our souls. (For further study in this area I recomend Jan Silvious's *Foolproofing Your Life: How to Deal Effectively with the Impossible People in Your Life.*)

Broken relationships hurt no matter how they occur. They can leave us wiped out, wounded, and desperately needing strength to take the next baby step down the road.

THE BROKEN ROAD

My first remembrance of a broken relationship is from the seventh grade. Several of my sixth-grade friends decided they'd like to be friends that year, just not with me. The upside was I learned how to make new friends that year. The downside was experiencing the severe pain of middle-school girl rejection.

What strengths have you developed that came at least in part from the pain of rejection?

Based on my own journey and recollections, I'm going to assume you have personally experienced a broken relationship sometime in your life too. If I'm wrong, I pray this week will equip you to love someone with the grace and strength of God.

Years ago, there was a line in a Rascal Flatts song that went like this: "God bless the broken road that led me straight to you." I still love that song and I guess millions of other people do too because the song becomes a hit for everyone who records it.

A lot of us know what it's like to walk a broken road. This past Christmas, my sweet husband bought the first real painting we've ever owned. Both of us had fallen in love with the work of Molly Courcelle (see *www.mollycourcelle.com*). It took forever, but we eventually narrowed our favorites to one. The name of our first venture into the world of art? *The Broken Road.*

I'm not sure it will do us much good to spend this week dredging up all the details of our brokenness. As you know, I was divorced. For seven years I was a single mom with four children. Scott and I married five years ago.

When I add it all up, the road I was assigned to walk for more than twenty years was severely broken. Since then I've asked God to help me forget most of it. Reliving the details makes my whole body ache. My stomach will start hurting and I'll feel so nauseated, I have to lie down. I don't want any of you sick at your stomach during Bible study, so let's approach this from a different angle. Instead of rehashing the pain, let's run after God for the healing.

Have you walked a broken road too? How tempting is it to rehash the details instead of searching for God's deep and abiding healing?

THE STRONGER HEALER

Right this second, you can Google the phrase "heal a broken heart" and begin reading page after page of fifteen ways, ten strategies, four surefire techniques, etc. My search reported 13,800,000 results. Who says this world doesn't have answers?

I clicked on three of the pages, all saying basically the same things. Nothing I read was bad advice, but most of it, in my opinion, was grossly mislabeled.

My search promised me healing strategies, but the content only delivered coping techniques. How to get by. Hang on. Make it another day.

Nothing is wrong with figuring how to make it through another day, but just don't call that healing. I want our broken places to be healed. We have a Stronger Healer and I know His promises are real.

> He heals the brokenhearted and binds up their wounds.
> Psalm 147:3

> The LORD is near to the brokenhearted and saves the crushed in spirit.
> Psalm 34:18

> He has sent me to bind up the brokenhearted.
> Isaiah 61:1

> But he was pierced for our transgressions; he was crushed for our iniquities; upon him was the chastisement that brought us peace, and with his wounds we are healed.
> Isaiah 53:5

> He himself bore our sins in his body on the tree, that we might die to sin and live to righteousness. By his wounds you have been healed.
> 1 Peter 2:24

In light of those verses, when you are broken, where is the Lord?

What does God do for the crushed in spirit?

Who bought our healing and how?

The Bible is true. God can heal you and me. Christ suffered and gave His life so that we can be healed. God has been faithful to keep His promises to me. My soul is being healed, not because of some well-applied coping strategies, but because God is stronger than my brokenness.

The Holy Spirit, who lives in me, is doing a miraculous work. He is teaching me the deeper places of God's truth. He is showing me what it means to apply His truth to my life. Day by day, He is providing the power to stay surrendered to God's ways and live a God-centered life. And here is the part I do not understand: with Christ at the center of my life, I experience healing in my soul.

Today, the question for us becomes the same one Jesus asked the invalid in John 5:6, "Do you want to be healed?"

Do you want to be healed? Tell Him your answer. Listen as He speaks.

A LITTLE STRONGER—I am tired of coping. I am tired of talking about my hurts. I am tired of living broken. I want to be healed.

MY BROKEN FRIENDSHIPS

As I've been praying about the broken friendships of women, I realize there are two different directions we might take with today's study. We could spend today recounting the details of our broken friendships—remembering who's to blame for what, thinking through scenarios and timelines, maybe even resurrecting the same grief and anger we've been holding onto for years.

The second option is for us to turn in the direction of God, asking Him to make us stronger than our broken friendships. Praise be to God, stronger is the direction we're taking today.

One note of advice before we begin. Some of you may need to talk through the details of a friendship that caused you great pain. Find someone you can speak to privately and confidentially—a counselor, pastor, or wise friend who is completely removed from your current circle of friends (especially not someone in this study group).

Don't forget to guard what and how you share from today's study. The aim of today is greater strength. We will all grieve if today becomes tainted with hints of gossip.

Let's pray.

Father, heal us. Heal all of us and make us stronger than we ever
thought we could be. In Jesus' mighty name. Amen.

HOW SHALL WE RESPOND?

When God begins making us stronger than our broken friendships, He changes the way we choose to respond to the person, the circumstances, and the hurt.

I'm hoping the passage you read next will challenge you right to your core. Jesus said:

> *A new commandment I give to you, that you love one another: just as I*
> *have loved you, you also are to love one another. By this all people will*
> *know that you are my disciples, if you have love for one another.*
> *John 13:34-35*

When Jesus makes us stronger than our broken friendships, He teaches us to respond in love just as He did, so the world will know we belong to Him.

List some of the ways you have previously responded to broken friendships.

1.

2.

3.

Now go back and put a big X over anything not done in the love of Christ. Do you get the feeling God is going to show us a new way?

JUST AS I HAVE LOVED YOU

This is not the passage I expected God to give me for today's topic. I was down the road toward a study about forgiveness, when it felt like God yelled, "More! Yes, yes, forgiveness, but there is more."

Reading Jesus' instruction to "Love one another just as I have loved you" with broken friendships in mind is stretching me in the best possible way. The Holy Spirit is tugging at my insides with such persistence, I know God wants you and me to get how big this is.

In physical strength-training, we stretch muscles beyond what we think they can do to build stronger muscles. That's exactly what the Lord is doing here. He is stretching our personal application of this passage to make us stronger. Let's revisit the last verse:

> *By this all people will know that you are my disciples, if you have love for one another.*
> *John 13:35*

Our life in Christ is to be lived as He lived, loving as He loved. The mandate here is to live so radically different we stand apart as His disciples. To respond and react to broken friendships with the love of Christ will seem irrational and shocking to this world because it is. Our world revolves around right and fair and correct. We protest to gain what we're entitled to. What's owed to us. What justice must be served. Jesus' kind of love is applied to this world in radically different ways.

Christ's command to love like He loves finds one of its most powerful life applications in our brokenness. To give the love of Christ in a broken friendship is a revolutionary idea. Look around and see how many people really live that kind of love. Certainly not enough.

Maybe you thought you signed up for the *Stronger* study, not a revolutionary life. But here's what I know. As we become stronger—learning to imitate the love of Christ to this broken world, loving in ways that are radically different—it will be revolutionary in your home, in your marriage, in your workplace, in your church, and in the hidden places of your heart. Loving as He loved can change everything.

Does your soul want to know more about this radical love business or are you hesitating? What are you feeling about all of this?

BROKEN FRIENDSHIP THROUGH EYES OF LOVE

Well, hmm. The love of Jesus is a really big thing. Big enough to cover you. Big enough to cover me. Is it big enough to cover the people in your broken friendships? I imagine the Holy Spirit is pounding on your heart about this, so while He's at work, I'll throw out a few ideas.

First, let's get a few things out of the way. Loving someone in a broken friendship does not mean doing any of the following:

- covering or minimizing the wrongs that have occurred
- restarting an unhealthy friendship or reconciling with a toxic person
- pretending to "love like Christ" for the sake of appearance
- allowing yourself to be manipulated, abused, or pressured

Seeing a broken friendship through the eyes of love means extending the same grace Christ has extended to you, the same mercy, the same forgiveness, and the same compassion. It means laying down our desire to condemn and to demand satisfaction, just as He laid down those things.

Loving a broken friend like Jesus loves you means doing the following:

- taking responsibility for your actions, your words, your part, your blind spots, and the things you have done wrong

- acknowledging any bitterness in your heart and deciding that bitterness will not guide your actions from here on out

- being open to reconciliation if it's possible

- asking God to soften your heart toward your friend's struggles, insecurities, and wounds, knowing that hurt people *hurt* people

- not gossiping to others about the disagreement with your friend

- remembering that we all need a Savior, often proving how desperately we still need Him

- lifting them up when they deserve your encouragement and you have the power to help

- stop spending energy and time focused on their offenses to you

- being open to God's power to change your heart toward the person

- being open to a different ending

- expecting nothing in return

- choosing the love of Christ even if it's returned with ungratefulness or selfishness

Go back over the list above. Beside each action item rate yourself with an A (if you're accomplishing the step with consistency), a G (if you really need to grow in that area), or a P (if you need to pray for willingness to work on that area).

After you've marked each item on the list, please write two or three action steps you will do this week.

When God makes us stronger, we surrender to living the truth of the Bible. When you consider your broken friendships, will you let the Scriptures be true in your life?

But love your enemies, and do good, and lend, expecting nothing in return, and your reward will be great, and you will be sons of the Most High, for he is kind to the ungrateful and the evil. Be merciful, even as your Father is merciful. Judge not, and you will not be judged; condemn not, and you will not be condemned; forgive, and you will be forgiven.
Luke 6:35-37

Be kind to one another, tenderhearted, forgiving one another, as God in Christ forgave you.
Ephesians 4:32

Above all, keep loving one another earnestly, since love covers a multitude of sins. Show hospitality to one another without grumbling.
1 Peter 4:8-9

Therefore let us not pass judgment on one another any longer.
Romans 14:13

A LITTLE STRONGER—The stronger response to broken friendships is to love as Christ loves me. More than forgiveness. More than distance. More than letting bygones be bygones. Love. Revolutionary, radical, Christ-like love.

The greatest "But God" verse of all time is this: "And when they had carried out all that was written of him, they took him down from the tree and laid him in a tomb. But God raised him from the dead" (Acts 13:29-30).

As a single mom, I realized my kids believed what I told them. If I said to them, "God has always taken care of us and He will never stop," they believed me. They lived as peaceful children, expecting God to come through, because I spoke God's truth instead of my fears over them.

DAY 3

MY BROKEN FAMILY

In today's study, we're going down a path I am all too familiar with. Being the mom of a broken family is my story. And maybe like you, belonging to a broken family was not a possibility I had ever considered. I did not grow up like this and never envisioned my home being the place of such brokenness and pain.

The abbreviated story of my journey includes almost fourteen years of marriage, the births of four children, separation, divorce, seven years as a single mom, remarriage, and then last year, the addition of our teenage, international son—also the child of a broken family.

Realizing I was going to become a divorced woman filled me with very deep shame, both personally and spiritually. What I'm going to say next may sound exaggerated and overly dramatic, but words don't exist to describe deep pain and its aftermath. My first marriage and divorce splintered my soul into thousands of pieces.

I've talked with other women who understand what it means to experience a soul-crushing. They also understand that afterward you learn to go numb. The crushed woman tries not to feel because feeling again might be more pain than she can bear. Thousands of splintered pieces stick and hurt and jab over and over, all day and all night.

On top of my personal brokenness, pressing down with great weight, were the souls and futures of my children. They were going to grow up in a very broken home. And my heart was filled with great fear.

Then Satan, who is a liar, rushed into my life with a vengeance. He screamed, yelled, and whispered to me through the night. He accused and condemned and told me worse things were coming. The main thing he wanted me to believe about my broken family was this: all hope was gone.

How does Satan try to rob you of hope?

People who mean well can say the dumbest things. People who don't know much about the love of God can issue judgments so strong and quick, they sound like they must be right. Folks on the Internet will provide you with statistics, true stories, and enough proof to convince you what you've heard about broken families is true. See if any of these sound familiar:

The individuals of broken families are destined to limp and struggle for the rest of their lives. The children will grow up to be criminals, or at least, underachievers and poor performers. Their future relationships are doomed to endure the same fate. Their lives will be marked by drug addiction and illicit sex. Unable to live at peace, each will spend a lifetime searching for the wholeness stolen by their broken family. And furthermore, God will not fellowship with the broken. He cannot use the broken. He will not allow the broken to lead or serve in His name. They still get to go to heaven, but His blessing on earth has been forfeited.

That's not all of it, but it's certainly enough to make my point.

If you believe what they say about broken families, then yes, all hope is gone. And when a crushed woman loses hope, then she becomes what they said would happen: another broken person who passes the pain to her children. I am certain that could have been me.

But God.

Many passages in the Bible show God intervening with His triumph over brokenness. This is one of my favorite:

But God, being rich in mercy, because of the great love with which he loved us, even when we were dead in our trespasses, made us alive together with Christ.
Ephesians 2:4-5

My broken life could have become another statistic or sad story, but God, who is rich in mercy, keeps His promises. He saved me a long time ago and He keeps saving me still. Sin and death cannot have the one who belongs to Christ. He keeps making us alive together in Christ.

When I became a follower of Jesus, I did not make that decision on a whim. I researched, read, and studied until I was convinced Jesus is the Son of God, full of power and full of grace. When I gave my life to Him, I gave Him everything and committed to believe Him wholeheartedly. With conscious intent, I decided to stake my whole life on the truth of Christ.

It would be dumb of me to disbelieve the statistics and stories about broken families because I see their truth all around me. But when my family became the broken story, I remembered the commitment I had made. I decided the only hope I had was to believe Jesus really is who He said He is. This crushed, broken woman whispered to God, *I still believe. I believe You are stronger than brokenness. I believe our only hope is in You.*

COVERED BY HIS MERCY

It has now been twelve years since my divorce. My family will not be finished needing the grace and mercy of Jesus until we are all finally home in His presence. But here is what I know for sure: God has covered this broken mom and her broken kids with His mercy. And when a family is covered by the powerful, merciful, sin-atoning, matchless blood of Jesus, the statistics do not apply. The power of God toward those who love Him and humble themselves before Him is stronger than the repercussions of brokenness and pain.

> *Having the eyes of your hearts enlightened, that you may know . . . what is the immeasurable greatness of his power toward us who believe, according to the working of his great might.*
> *Ephesians 1:18-19*

When we humble ourselves under the covering of His mercy, God glorifies Himself, even in broken families. Placing my family under the covering of God's mercy meant (1) doing whatever I had to do to keep Christ at the center of our lives, (2) doing whatever I had to do to keep Satan outside of our house, and (3) keeping my heart open and ready to be changed and redirected by His grace.

What practical steps could you take today to place your family under the cover of God's mercy?

A LITTLE STRONGER—A family may break, but God's love never does. In my darkest place, I will put my trust in the power of the One I have believed.

MY BROKEN DREAMS

True confession. Walt Disney World is one of my favorite places on the planet. I do realize this confession may divide us. Either you just rolled your eyes over my lack of intellect and my ridiculous whimsy or you ran to find your personalized ears. The non-Disney folks will not understand.

As a girl, I loved every vacation my family spent at Disney World. As a mom, my Disney love has not diminished. How could anyone resist? Magic days filled with helpful attendants, larger-than-life characters, rides, funnel cakes, fairy dust, and happy endings.

Even better, all that fun comes wrapped in a promise. Everyone who walks through the turnstiles is promised their dreams can come true. It's a very fancy notion in a fantasy world, designed to lift your spirits and provide a few moments away from your burdens. And it does.

You may not feel the same way about Disney World, but I wonder if you've ever hummed along to this catchy tune:

> *When you wish upon a star*
> *Makes no difference who you are*
> *Anything your heart desires*
> *Will come to you*

Though it's a misguided notion, we want to believe the fantasy that anything your heart desires will come to you.

How about you? Ever sing along, hoping the song might be true?

WHEN A DREAM IS A WISH YOUR HEART MAKES

Did the following pattern happen in your life?

- Somewhere along the way, you let yourself dream like a Disney princess. The wishes your heart made became your dreams.

• Many of those dreams from your heart are now broken and gone.

• The list of your broken dreams makes it hard to believe God is interested in your joy.

I have been reading Dr. Larry Crabb's *Shattered Dreams*. One of the first things he teaches concerns God's heart toward us. Read this excerpt and then answer the questions that follow.

> *There's never a moment in all our lives, from the day we first trusted Christ till the day we see Him, when God is not longing to bless us. At every moment, in every circumstance, God is doing us good . . . At this exact moment, He is giving us what He thinks is good.*[1]

Whatever is going on for you today, which of these represent your awareness of God's good heart toward you?

_____ *When I look at my broken dreams, I can't see or feel any of God's blessing toward me.*

_____ *God may be giving me what is good for me, but I don't like it.*

_____ *God is doing me good, and I'm learning to believe that more and more.*

Here is a truth we sometimes find hard to believe: God is always doing good for us. He is behind the scenes plotting for our joy. In fact, the entire Book of Ruth is a beautiful picture of God's plotting for good, even when everything seems broken. He takes pleasure in blessing us and giving us what He determines is for our good.

Now, let's change gears for a minute. What are your five greatest pleasures on this earth?

1.

2.

3.

4.

5.

Before we continue, read a few more words from Dr. Crabb:

> *We can't stop wanting to be happy. And that urge should prompt no apology. We were created for happiness. Our souls therefore long for whatever we think will provide the greatest possible pleasure. We just aren't yet aware that an intimate relationship with God is that greatest pleasure.*[2]

Did you catch that last sentence? We just aren't yet aware that an intimate relationship with God is our greatest pleasure.

For much of my life, my relationship with God did not make my Greatest Pleasure list. I have loved the Lord all this time, yet did not understand how my relationship with Him could bring greater joy than anything else my heart desired. Somehow, I kept my earthly pleasures and my relationship with God on separate lists.

Psalm 16:11 makes it very plain: the greatest joy we can know is joy in the Lord:

> *"You make known to me the path of life; in your presence there is fullness of joy; at your right hand are pleasures forevermore."*

For all who belong to God, Scripture promises fullness of joy and pleasures forevermore in His presence. We are in His presence when we have an intimate relationship with Him. Full, eternal joy cannot be improved. You cannot be fuller than full or last longer than forevermore! God alone is the source of our full and lasting pleasure.

How's your awareness of pleasure in relationship with Him?
___ This is the first day I have ever considered the possibility of God being my greatest pleasure.

___ I have heard some of this before and half-heartedly believed there might be more joy in God than anything. I guess other things have distracted me from living in the strength of this truth.

___ I have gotten to this truth the hard way, but I can say with confidence that my relationship with God is the source of my greatest pleasure.

Is there a possibility that many of our dreams were just the wishes of our hearts, instead being the dreams given from the intimacy of God's presence?

When I consider that question, my honest answer is yes. Many of my past dreams were determined with my earthly pleasure and my happiness in mind. How about you?

It turns out, I settled for the lower dreams my heart made. In order to know God's greater good and higher dreams, many of my lower dreams had to be broken.

Do you remember any of the lower dreams your heart settled for?

Have any of those lower dreams become your broken dreams?

IT'S OK TO DREAM

My sister-in-law is amazing. If called her on the phone right this minute and said, "Quick, tell me your top five hopes and dreams," she could do it. She would zip through that list like she had been waiting for me to call. The girl knows her dreams and she knows her heart's desires.

I, on the other hand, am not well acquainted with my hopes and dreams. I can't hand you a list, and it would be painful if you asked me to make one. My lack of dreams is probably a by-product of my brokenness, but lately I have decided a woman shouldn't be without dreams. When I finish writing this study, there are a lot of things on my to-do list, but one of them is to spend time in prayer and study, asking God about His dreams for me. Asking Him to put His dreams in my heart.

A broken life is full of broken dreams. And broken women learn to stop dreaming. That sounds kind of awful until you realize God uses broken dreams to help us begin dreaming His dreams for our lives.

God is teaching me it's OK to dream and hope and wish again. But this time, He is calling me to higher dreams. His.

Does your broken heart need permission to dream again? If so, start by telling yourself you are done with lower dreams. You will not settle for anything less than God's higher standard. Does your soul need a time of prayer and seeking? See if you can relate to the following ideas:

• I know God is telling me to lay down my dreams and start over. I have dreamed only of myself and now I realize there is more.

• There are no dreams left in me. All I've ever had are broken. But I hear God giving me permission to dream, so I will seek Him.

• I am eager to take my dreams into God's presence, holding each one up for Him to examine. And I am willing to lay down everything not high enough for His glory.

A LITTLE STRONGER—God's dreams for me are higher and stronger than the dreams I have for myself. My journey toward His greater good might be through broken dreams, but I will trust Him.

MY EASTER SUNDAY GOD

I began working on this study about eighteen months ago. The manuscript was due to my LifeWay editor, Dale McCleskey, exactly five months ago. My schedule was cleared for writing and my intentions were good, but none of us anticipated my mom's illness or my parent's move to our home, and the too soon home-going of my mama.

To this very day, the team at LifeWay has covered me with their prayers, giving me nothing but grace and encouragement. But still, I desperately wanted to make up the lost time in my writing. When my work is late to them, I cause twenty more people to miss deadlines and stay up later to work longer. My late work puts more stress on their desks, and I can't stand the thought of adding to their burdens.

Hard as I tried in these past five months, I could not overcome the lost time. I love my family with all my heart and I have always tried to show them with my actions that nothing matters more than they do. So if it hadn't been for the orthodontist, visits with my dad, soccer games, carpool, and making dinner, these words might have been written a little sooner.

So this study is being finished in the week leading up to Easter. On Monday I wanted to be done by Wednesday, but so many family things interrupted my plans. Then I hoped for Thursday. Maybe Good Friday. But here I am on Saturday, late in the night, just a few hours until Easter Sunday. Sometime this afternoon, I began to see God's plan unfolding.

I am writing the last day of this study, anticipating the celebration of Easter Sunday tomorrow morning. Now I can see very clearly that God intended for these last words to be written tonight. And I am grateful. Humbled by His delays. Honored to be writing about His strength and His glory this holy night, on these holy days.

WHEN IT'S STILL FRIDAY IN YOUR HEART

Last night, Scott and I attended the Good Friday service at our church. My pastor, Don Miller, walked us through the timeline of Holy Week. We worshiped and prayed and reflected on the last days before Christ's crucifixion. I was doing pretty good until communion. Scott and I walked up to take the elements, then we knelt together at the altar to pray. And when we bent down to pray, I remembered my mama. And all of a sudden, I could see her in my mind. There she was in heaven with Jesus. Stronger.

That is exactly why He had to die.

Jesus died so she could be forgiven of her sins and saved from the penalty of death. Given a new body and a new home. Enjoying the presence of the Savior forever. Happy. Redeemed. Alive, not dead. She's alive because He died.

Christ died that Friday to prove He was stronger than everything. But for those who waited, Friday seemed like the end. Where was the strength? Where was the glory? Surely all hope was gone. Remember E.V. Hill's powerful sermon about that Friday? Part of it went like this:

> *It's Friday. Jesus is arrested in the garden where He was praying. But Sunday's coming. It's Friday. The disciples are hiding and Peter's denying that he knows the Lord. But Sunday's coming.*
> *It's Friday. Jesus is standing before the high priest of Israel, silent as a lamb before the slaughter. But Sunday's coming.*
> *It's Friday. Jesus is beaten, mocked, and spit upon. But Sunday's coming . . .*
> *And on that horrible day 2,000 years ago, Jesus the Christ, the Lord of glory, the only begotten Son of God, the only perfect man died on the cross of Calvary. Satan thought that he had won the victory . . . But that was Friday.[3]*

Maybe today feels like Friday in your heart. The sky is dark. Your dreams are dying. Hope is gone. Satan is laughing. And you sit in your Friday darkness wondering, *Where is this God who promises He is stronger?*

My sweet friend, if I could reach out and take your hand, I would. I'd share your tears and brush the hair from your eyes. Then I'd whisper, "Hold on. I know it feels like Friday in your soul, but oh, hallelujah, Sunday's a-coming."

MY EASTER SUNDAY GOD

The E.V. Hill sermon continues:

> *It's Sunday, and the crucified and resurrected Christ has defeated death, hell, sin, and the grave. It's Sunday. And now everything has changed. It's the age of grace, God's grace poured out on all who would look to that crucified lamb of Calvary. Grace freely given to all who would believe that Jesus Christ died on the cross of Calvary, was buried, and rose again. All because it's Sunday.[4]*

If ever you are tempted to think God is not big enough, He is not close enough, He could not love you enough, I want you to remember this one thing: the Lord, who is stronger than everything, is our Easter Sunday God. On that day, by the death and resurrection of His Son, God proved for once and for all the glory of His power.

He is stronger than death. Greater than our sin. More faithful than we may ever understand.

Because of that first Easter, all who believe Jesus died that dark Friday and rose victorious on Sunday are freely given the grace to live stronger in Him.

Oh, my friend, the clock by my bed has now ticked past midnight. It's Easter Sunday here. My heart swells with gratefulness for the life He gave. My tears flow, rejoicing in the truth of Christ's sacrifice for us. Will you believe Him today? Will you give Him your weakness and your sin? Will you ask Him to be victorious in your struggles?

He is our great Easter Sunday God.

He is stronger than everything. Hallelujah. Amen and amen.

A LITTLE STRONGER—For too many days I have lived in the darkness of Good Friday. By God's grace, I commit to live in the glory of my Easter Sunday God. He is stronger and oh, hallelujah, I am HIS.

VIEWER GUIDE SESSION 7

PSALM 84

UNTIL WE'RE HOME

Hebrews 12:2

As pilgrims in this world, on this journey toward our _____ _____, the one thing we know for sure is that, one day, we will be _____.

Let's look at the _____ and how He _____ running this race.

LOOK TO JESUS

He is both the _____ of this journey that I am making with Him and He is the _____.

KEEP HIM IN THE CENTER

Imitate what He has done for me to _____ the _____.

Endure on your _____ what comes at you.

NOTES

WEEK 1

1. A. W. Tozer, *The Knowledge of the Holy* (New York: HarperCollins, 1978), 74.
2. C. H. Spurgeon, "The Immutability of God" (sermon, New Park Street Chapel, Southwark, London, January 7, 1855).
3. Ibid.
4. W. A. Grudem, *Systematic Theology* (Grand Rapids, MI: Zondervan, 1994), 191.
5. Tozer, 56.
6. Richard Watson, *A Biblical and Theological Dictionary* (New York: B. Waugh and T. Mason, 1832), 43.
7. Arthur Pink, (CreateSpace Independent Publishing Platform, 2012), 55.
8. Tozer, 1.
9. Tullian Tchividjian, *Jesus + Nothing = Everything* (Wheaton, IL: Crossway, 2011), 53.
10. Charles Swindoll, *Saying It Well* (Nashville: FaithWords, 2012), 92.
11. Francis Chan, *Crazy Love* (Colorado Springs: David C. Cook, 2008), 168.
12. Steve Brown from Key Life radio.
13. Jerry Bridges, *Trusting God* (Colorado Springs: NavPress, 2008), 198.
14. Ibid, 21.

WEEK 2

1. You can read more about this research in *Bowling Alone: The Collapse and Revival of American Community* by Robert D. Putnam, Touchstone Books, 2001.
2. Stephen Marche. "Is Facebook Making Us Lonely?" *Atlantic Magazine,* May 2012, *http://www.theatlantic.com/magazine/archive/2012/05/is-facebook-making-us-lonely/308930/.*
3. C. H. Spurgeon, "Christ's Loneliness and Ours" (sermon, no further information offered).
4. K. S. Wuest, "Hebrews 13:5," *Wuest's Word Studies from the Greek New Testament: For the English Reader* (Grand Rapids: Eerdmans, 1997).
5. J. D. Barry and R. Kruyswijk, "Connect the Testaments: A Daily Devotional" (Bellingham, WA: Logos Bible Software, 2012).
6. P. L. Tan, *Encyclopedia of 7700 Illustrations: Signs of the Times* (Garland, TX: Bible Communications, Inc, 1996).
7. Lee Strobel, *The Case for Faith* (Grand Rapids, MI: Zondervan, 2000), 226.
8. C. H. Spurgeon, "Mr. Fearing Comforted" (sermon, New Park Street Chapel, April 3, 1859).
9. Ibid.
10. Ibid.
11. Andrew Murray, *The Wisdom of Andrew Murray* (Radford, VA: Wilder Publications, 2008), 35.

WEEK 3

1. John Eldredge, *Beautiful Outlaw* (New York: FaithWords, 2011), 61.

2. W. A. Elwell and B. J. Beitzel, *Baker Encyclopedia of the Bible* (Grand Rapids, MI: Baker Book House, 1988), 765.

3. G. C. Jones, *1000 Illustrations for Preaching and Teaching* (Nashville, TN: Broadman & Holman Publishers, 1986), 155.

4. C. H. Spurgeon, "Though He Were Dead" (sermon, Metropolitan Tabernacle, Newington, September 14, 1884).

5. Jones, 102.

6. P. L. Tan, *Encyclopedia*.

7. Ibid.

8. Jones, 102.

WEEK 5

1. Wayne Grudem, *Systematic Theology* (Grand Rapids, MI: Zondervan, 1994), 747–48.

2. Tchividjian, 77.

3. For entire poem, see *http://www.bartleby.com/236/239.html*.

WEEK 6

1. Larry Crabb, *Shattered Dreams* (Colorado Springs, CO: WaterBrook Press, 2001), 1.

2. Ibid, 2.

3. See *http://apologetica.us/2009/04/10/its-friday-but-sundays-coming-2/*.

4. Ibid.

LEADER GUIDE

Thank you for leading the study of *Stronger*. This brief leader guide offers some ideas, but I urge you to rely on the Holy Spirit for true guidance. These are only suggestions.

Let's start with the order of events in group study: you first study the week of print material on a topic, then watch the video, and finally share in a small group. For the first week your group will watch the Session 1 video and do some basic group building. Then members will study Week 1 in preparation for Session 2.

To prepare for leading each week, complete the study and preview the video. Set up the meeting room, including the necessary equipment. The suggested questions in this leader guide come from the week's study or build upon the week's study. They are intended to be discussion starters.

SESSION 1

Use the first session to build fellowship in your group. Familiarize yourself with the contents of the study. Preview the study for the members, so they will know what is expected each week. Watch the Session 1 video and ask members what they hope to gain from your time together. (Note: In all other sessions, each session's Viewer Guide is found on the **page before** the session begins.) Here are some additional suggestions:

1. Have women introduce and tell something about themselves.

2. Direct members to the table of contents on page 3. Ask which topics they are eager about and which they are hesitant about.

3. Encourage group members to be honest and to maintain absolute confidentiality, as you will be talking about sensitive topics.

4. Be sure each woman gets a copy of *Stronger: Finding Hope in Fragile Places* and instruct them to complete Week 1.

5. Gather and distribute contact information for the group.

6. Pray that God will make you stronger in Him. Consider having prayer partners for the duration of group.

SESSION 2

Preview the video session. Welcome group members and pray. Begin either by sharing some of the response to their study this week or by viewing the video. Then, as time permits, discuss some of the following questions from the first week's study.

1. What characteristics of God did you record on page 10? Why are those characteristics particularly important to you?

2. Is your first reaction to God's ubiquity "Oh no, I can never escape Him" or "Oh yes, He'll never leave me"?

3. What unchanging item did you draw on page 12?

4. Has God been present even where you would not have expected Him in your life? How (p. 13)?

5. How does the omniscience of God give you comfort? How does that truth make you tremble (p. 16)?

6. Do you agree with the statement on page 20: "To believe God loves you is crucial to our journey in this life." Why or why not?

7. How is the idea that you or I am uniquely unforgiveable an expression of misguided pride (p. 22)?

8. With no worrying about right or wrong answers, how would you respond to the question, How does one receive the strength of God (p. 25)?

9. What kind of strength do you think God gives to those who stay near Him (p. 28)?

10. Why do you think so many believers still live in tragic weakness (p. 30)?

11. What examples did you cite of biblical characters wanting God's strength only on their own terms (p. 33)?

12. On page 35, what are some ways you might fill in the blank: My _____ + God's strength = God's glory?

SESSION 3

Preview the video in preparation for the session. Welcome group members and pray. Begin either by sharing some of the response to their study this week or by viewing the video. Then, as time permits, discuss some of the following questions from the second week's study.

1. What details of your loneliest time made the situation even more difficult (p. 38)?

2. What action can you take to fortify yourself against loneliness (p. 41)?

3. What steps from Day 2 can you exercise in dealing with temptation (p. 49)?

4. How would you describe the stressors in your life (p. 52)?

5. All kinds of things in this world promise to give you peace. What is the difference between worldly peace and divine peace (p. 53)?

6. How would you complete the truth statement from page 55: This _____ is _____. But God is _____.

7. Do you struggle with any of the reasons for doubt listed on page 58? If not, what causes your doubt?

8. How might changing your perspective aid you in dealing with doubt (p. 60)?

9. How has God surprised you with a sharp turn in your road (p. 62)?

10. We all need to humble ourselves over and over. What situation do you face now that challenges you to humble yourself (p. 64)?

11. How would you explain the statement by St. Augustine: "Love God and do what you please" (p. 65)?

SESSION 4

Welcome group members and pray. Begin either by sharing some of the response to their study this week or by viewing the video. Then, as time permits, discuss some of the following questions from the third week's study.

1. What effects of living in this broken world are troubling you most these days (p. 70)?

2. How has God shown you peace in the midst of tribulation (p. 74)?

3. Are people you know asking God how long and why (p. 77)? What about?

4. How do you respond when life's unfair, good guys lose, or disease comes (p. 78)?

5. Why did Habakkuk say he would rejoice even in the most trying of times (p. 79)?

6. How does the joy of our salvation give us strength to rejoice, even when the worst thing happens (p. 79)?

7. What characteristics have you seen in a person battling disease and still trusting God (p. 80)?

8. Which Scripture that you paraphrased on pages 84–85 spoke most to you?

9. Have you seen an occasion in which one believer's faith through a tragedy impacted others (p. 87)? What happened?

10. What gifts from trusting God did you identify in the Scriptures (pp. 88–89)?

11. Consider the self-rating of your trust in God on page 89. What steps could you take to increase your trust in Him?

SESSION 5

Welcome group members and pray. Begin either by sharing some of the response to their study this week or by viewing the video. Then, as time permits, discuss some of the following questions from the fourth week's study.

1. Why do we so often get stuck in the comparison game (p. 93)?

2. If you live with task overload, what have you added to make the burden even heavier (p. 94)?

3. What do you think God is saying to you about task overload and the attitudes it brings (pp. 94–95)?

4. Why do we sometimes feel saying no is un-Christian (pp. 95–96)?

5. What distractions do you need to learn to control (p. 98)?

6. What would it mean to "set your face like flint" concerning the distractions you could learn to control (p. 99)?

7. What does your unrealistic magazine dream look like (p. 101)?

8. How have your unrealistic expectations of someone else (to complete you, always keep promises, or be your Savior) impacted your life (p. 102)?

9. If you let yourself and others off the hook of unrealistic expectations, how might that change your life (p. 104)?

10. Why do we search for an elusive life balance in unrealistic ways (p. 106)?

11. In what ways do you look more like the image of Jesus this year than you ever have (p. 110)?

12. For what did you find yourself praying in Day 5 (pp. 111–115)?

SESSION 6

Welcome group members and pray. Begin either by sharing some of the response to their study this week or by viewing the video. Then, as time permits, discuss some of the following questions from the fifth week's study.

1. What difference does it makes to commit to obedience before you spend time with God (p. 118)?

2. In what ways were we all dead before Christ made us alive (p. 120)? What are some of your particular "dead places" (p. 121)?

3. In what ways have you struggled with thinking too much of yourself? What insight did you gain from the four case studies of how girls grow up to deal with attitudes toward self (p. 124)?

4. How have you dealt with self-focus? How has this changed through the years (p. 124)?

5. What's the difference between healthy and unhealthy ways of thinking about self (p. 125)?

6. What spiritual moral did you draw from the story of the woman who stopped yelling (p. 127)?

7. If you could stop thinking about yourself too much, what kind of woman might you become (p. 127)?

8. What practical difference might remembering your name/citizenship/number make? What practical difference might remembering your citizenship make? What practical difference might remembering your number make (p. 130)?

9. How can we discern the difference between a healthy desire to serve and a pathological need to please (p. 133)?

10. Why do you think women struggle with wanting to be loved by everybody? As a group, list as many reasons as possible (p. 133).

11. What would becoming a woman who lives in the full assurance of God's approval and acceptance change about you (p. 136)? In your home? Relationships? Everyday life?

SESSION 7

Welcome group members and pray. Begin either by sharing some of the response to their study this week or by viewing the video. Then, as time permits, discuss some of the following questions from the final week's study.

1. Why do you suppose Proverbs says so much about relationships with fools (p. 145)?

2. How did you summarize in one sentence the teaching of the Proverbs concerning fools (p. 145)?

3. What strengths have you developed that came at least in part from the pain of rejection (p. 145)?

4. What does God do for the crushed in spirit? Who bought our healing and how (p. 147)?

5. What are some ways you've responded to broken friendships (p. 150)?

6. After completing the activities on page 152, what insights or actions have you made a priority for yourself this week?

7. What practical steps could you take today to place and keep your family under the cover of God's mercy (p. 156)?

8. Whatever is going on for you today, which response on page 158 represents your awareness of God's good heart toward you?

9. How would you explain to a new believer what Dr. Larry Crabb means by the statement, "An intimate relationship with God is the greatest pleasure" (p. 159)?

Thank you for leading *Stronger*. Encourage your group to celebrate the reality that God's strength comes to the humble and those who are most aware of their weakness. We can always depend on God's promise that He "opposes the proud, but gives grace to the humble" (James 4:6; 1 Peter 5:5). Stronger always means His grace rather than our independence.